grace
in the middle

Grace in the Middle has just ranked as one of my all-time favorite books—EVER. You will laugh out loud and cry empathetic tears. But there's a story within the story that every believer must tackle for the sake of their own faith; Surrender. "I want to know Him in the power of His resurrection, and in the fellowship of His sufferings" (Phil 3:10). The Holy Spirit will minister to you through Wendy's "fellowship of His sufferings," and if you're willing . . . it will change your life!

—Rachel Lee Carter
Author of *Fashioned by Faith* (Thomas Nelson, 2011),
Founder of Modeling Christ Ministries

This book touched me deeply. I sat down one night thinking I would just read a few chapters, but I couldn't put it down and finished in one sitting. Throughout the story I found God speaking to me in so many areas that challenged me to examine my relationship with my entire family and most importantly, with Him. The story is an honest look at heartbreak and joy at the same time. It's okay to say "life is hard." Sometimes life doesn't make sense, but Wendy's mad writing skills bring things into perspective. Sometimes men will see a book by a female author and think it's a chick book. This book is for everyone!

—Darrell Cothran
Minister of Media,
First Baptist North Spartanburg

How do we react when tragedy unexpectedly rears it ugly head into our lives? Who do we lean on? Who do we become? Wendy and Scott Duke saw their world collapse around them when they heard some frightening news regarding their unborn daughter, but, through it all, they never let go of God, and, most importantly, God never let go of them. This is a must-read book for all of us who have hit tough times in our lives. Wendy shows us in *Grace In The Middle*, that even when there is tragedy, there is also faith, hope, and above all else, love.

—Brett Parks
Author of *Miracle Man: A Bullet That Ignited a Purpose-Filled Life*,
Founder and President of Second Shot Ministry

Honest, raw, and deeply compelling, *Grace in the Middle* is a book for anyone who's ever felt powerless, who's wondered, *Where is God in all of this?* Wendy Duke lays bare the road from heartbreak to hope, from spiritual numbness to powerful faith. In Savannah's strength, determination, and resilience, readers will find their own.

—Lisa Wingate
National Bestselling Author of *The Prayer Box*
and *The Sea Keeper's Daughters*

What a terrific reminder of God's grace and love and provision and steadfastness and . . . well, everything HE says in HIS word. Get this book by Wendy Duke, in fact, get it and get another to give to a friend!

—Mickey Henderson
Pastor of Spiritual Development,
Sunnyvale First Baptist Church, Sunnyvale, TX

Grace in the Middle is a MUST-READ for all moms! Wendy Duke beautifully describes the hope that can be found in Jesus regardless of our personal circumstances. Every mom will be blessed to experience this journey filled with struggles leading to the profound mercy of God's sovereignty that is available to each one of us. Wendy is a skilled writer who uses her stones of remembrance of God's faithfulness to issue a tender call for full surrender to God.

—Chimene Shipley Dupler
President/CEO of Passion4Moms
www.passion4moms.org

grace
in the middle

AN IMPERFECT JOURNEY
TO GOD'S PERFECT PLAN

wendy duke

AMBASSADOR INTERNATIONAL
GREENVILLE, SOUTH CAROLINA & BELFAST, NORTHERN IRELAND

www.ambassador-international.com

Grace in the Middle
An Imperfect Journey to God's Perfect Plan

ISBN: 978-1-62020-529-7
eISBN: 978-1-62020-436-8

Unless otherwise indicated, Scripture Quotations from THE HOLY BIBLE, NEW INTERNATIONAL VERSION®, NIV® Copyright © 1973, 1978, 1984, 2011 by Biblica, Inc.® Used by permission. All rights reserved worldwide.

Scripture marked GW is taken from GOD'S WORD®, © 1995 God's Word to the Nations. Used by permission of Baker Publishing Group.

Cover Design and Page Layout by Hannah Nichols
eBook Conversion by Anna Raats

AMBASSADOR INTERNATIONAL
Emerald House
427 Wade Hampton Blvd.
Greenville, SC 29609, USA
www.ambassador-international.com

AMBASSADOR BOOKS
The Mount
2 Woodstock Link
Belfast, BT6 8DD, Northern Ireland, UK
www.ambassadormedia.co.uk

The colophon is a trademark of Ambassador

To my husband, Scott,
and my children, Savannah and JP,
for your sacrifices and encouragement.
Your opinions of me are the
only ones that matter.

NOTE FROM THE AUTHOR:

This book is an updated edition of my first work entitled The Grace by Which We Stand, published in 2008. This edition contains a new chapter and six years' worth of reflection and new stories to tell.

W.D.

CONTENTS

PREFACE 11

CHAPTER 1
BABY 15

CHAPTER 2
BEARING BAD NEWS 33

CHAPTER 3
PREPARING FOR BATTLE 43

CHAPTER 4
WHEN THE EARTH GIVES WAY 63

CHAPTER 5
THROUGH THE FIRE 71

CHAPTER 6
SHADE TREES 81

CHAPTER 7
THE FIRST WAVE 99

CHAPTER 8
SUNSHINE ON OUR FACES 111

CHAPTER 9

THE BACK SIDE OF THE STORM   115

CHAPTER 10

JUST ONE STEP   125

CHAPTER 11

WHILE WE WAIT   135

CHAPTER 12

ON THE WATER   149

CHAPTER 13

KEEP MOVING   167

CHAPTER 14

THROUGH SAVANNAH'S EYES   181

ACKNOWLEDGEMENTS   189

ABOUT THE AUTHOR   191

PREFACE

And Joshua set up at Gilgal the twelve stones they had taken out of the Jordan. He said to the Israelites, "In the future when your descendants ask their parents 'What do these stones mean,' tell them, 'Israel crossed the Jordan on dry ground.' For the Lord your God dried up the Jordan before you until you had crossed over. The Lord your God did to the Jordan just what he had done to the Red Sea when he dried it up before us until we had crossed over. He did this so that all the peoples of the earth might know that the hand of the LORD is powerful and so that you might always revere the LORD your God."

~ Joshua 4: 20–24

SINCE JANUARY 2000, THE BACKGROUND music of my life has been set to the melody of my daughter, Savannah. The circumstances surrounding her birth and first few years of life have been extraordinary, to say the least, life-changing in ways that are hard to write down. Her life has shaped mine in so many ways.

Many of my friends and some strangers encouraged me to write "Savannah's story." To be honest, I did everything in my power *not* to write this story. I discovered that diving back into that season of my life was more difficult than I ever imagined. The process of writing dredged up memories I had long tried to forget, opened up wounds I thought had healed. It was painful and entirely frightening.

God and I went head-to-head over this. Like the story of Jacob in Genesis 32:22, we wrestled hard. He is a fierce opponent, I tell you, and not intimidated by me at all. But utterly kind He is, and His intention was not to break me but to hold my undivided attention and trust. In all this wrestling, I tasted the holy privilege of being wrapped in the arms of the Living God, even if it was while He pinned me to the ground. Sometimes I need to be reminded I'm not nearly as big or strong as I think I am. Pride needed to be broken. But even His strength is tucked inside the folds of mercy, and His gentle voice was ever in my ear: *I'm on your side. We'll do this together.*

I walk around with a bit of a holy limp now. It is a constant reminder of my smallness in the face of the Great I Am and the delight He finds in me as His beloved.

The New Testament is rich with encounters Jesus had with everyday people, people whose lives were changed dramatically after coming face to face with the Redeemer of the world: blind men given sight; a broken woman spared humiliation and punishment; real people freed from the chains of lifelong disabilities; children healed of sickness; people brought from death to life. In almost all of those accounts, the one whose life intersected with Jesus immediately ran and told anyone who would listen. They gave testimony to the impact He'd had on their lives. So I'm just going to follow that lead.

This story isn't really about my daughter. Savannah, my husband, and I play supporting roles, but this is the story of a God who is greater than medicine and logic and religion, a God who is small enough to show up in a hospital room with a baby girl and her mama and daddy. This is the story of a God who sees us, who cares, who doesn't stumble, and who never leaves us, even if we ask Him to.

This is also a portrait of grace, that mysterious abstraction we sing about on Sunday mornings but don't know how to put into words. I discovered the essence of it as God made His way to me, pushing past the wreckage of broken walls and shattered faith. This story is an unwrapping of the relentless Creator's love poured over me in the lowest, ugliest moments of my life. His grace pulled me up from despair and looming defeat. It set me on solid ground, dusted me off, and sent me back into the game, but stronger, more seasoned, more solid. I want to tell you the story of my God and the mighty long way He has brought me since my daughter was born, because I want you to know that He *is* who He says He is. This is my honest account of the wonder God has worked in me and for my family, because I know there is someone out there somewhere who is hurting, wounded, and ready to give up. I want you to know that He is the God who sees you and is waiting for your call. Whatever you need, He can do it. Whatever storm you are battling, He is in the middle of it, waiting for you to find refuge in Him as waves and winds swirl. Without Him, we cannot stand.

CHAPTER 1

BABY

For I am the Lord, your God, who takes hold of your right hand
and says to you, Do not fear; I will help you.
Do not be afraid.

~ Isaiah 41:13-14a

THERE ARE MOMENTS IN LIFE that take your breath away. And
then there are moments that suck all of the air out of the room.

We had been here before. Well, not this room exactly, but they're
all pretty much the same. A small, narrow room lined with an assort-
ment of wood-framed chairs and patterned carpet underfoot. The
décor strokes the estrogen-tinted eye: muted pinks and greens, floral
and plaid cushions on a loveseat, and the last several months' issues
of *Better Homes & Garden* and *American Baby* magazines stacked neatly
on the side tables. This was our first layover in this particular waiting
room—a different office, a different stage in our lives and marriage,
a different pregnancy—but it was the same. Same butterflies in the
stomach; same vulnerable tightrope of high hopes and total absence
of control. We had been here before.

Our previous three pregnancies had all started in the same place and ended in heartbreak.

The first one was a surprise. We had been married two years and were both shocked when a round of antibiotics chiseled a hole in the armor wide enough to usher in two little lines on a pregnancy test six weeks later. We were excited but had no idea how this thing worked. The morning sickness and other symptoms were novel and oddly exciting; there was something weirdly validating about throwing up in the mornings, like some kind of gruesome trophy with the inscription: *Yes, you are indeed with child.* Our house was peppered with pregnancy literature and books, and I'd already bought some maternity clothes, even though nobody could tell I was pregnant yet.

At fourteen weeks along, Scott and I chatted nervously in the paisley upholstered chairs, naïve youngsters with goofy grins on our faces in the obstetrician's waiting room for our first visit. After being led back to a small ultrasound room, I lay on the vinyl table and Scott stood beside me as the technician wielded her "probe" and we searched the screen for tiny body parts.

"Have you had any morning sickness or other symptoms?" she asked.

"Yes, I'm sick a couple of days a week," I answered. If I were standing, I probably would have raised my chin and puffed out my chest.

The technician didn't speak anymore except to ask me how far along I was—again. We recounted our calculations and waited for her affirmation, but the room fell heavy with silence. Then she clipped, "Wait here. I need to find the doctor." My heart started pounding. Scott, the eternal optimist, tried to tell me that this was probably normal; surely the doctor would need to check everything out at every ultrasound. But when the doctor came in, I knew. Something was wrong.

He was too calm, too quiet; his smile had too much effort in it. He and the technician talked in hushed gibberish for a few minutes before he turned the screen to us and showed us a small white spot.

"This is the fetal pole," he pointed. "The baby should form arm and leg buds here at about seven or eight weeks. The heartbeat can be seen as early as five weeks, but definitely by week ten. According to your timeline, you should be at least fourteen weeks along. Unfortunately, we don't see a heartbeat here, and no growth of the arm or leg buds. It looks as if your baby's demise occurred at around eight weeks."

Just like that. We sat in stunned silence for a few minutes. I don't know what else he said. I don't remember the rest of the day. I vaguely remember driving back to the hospital for the D&E to remove the remains of the baby a few days later and then crying all the way home.

A pathology report of the tissue showed that our baby had a chromosomal disorder called Trisomy 18, a condition that results in extreme birth defects of the arms and legs as well as an underdeveloped brain and a very short life span. If we had another baby, we were at greater risk that it would have the same chromosomal disorder, although the percentage was small. But neither of us was ready to try this again. Not for a while, anyway.

My husband and I were both high school teachers and basketball coaches, so we threw ourselves back into our world of practices and road games and lesson plans and practice drills and paper-grading and whistle-blowing. The life of a coach is hard on families—we were up early, home late, and free time was spent doing glamorous things like watching game films. We spent four nights a week at ball games, either coaching or watching each other's team play. So when we lost the baby, we comforted ourselves by saying the timing probably wasn't right, that we were too busy to start a family. That our careers were just starting to take off. We nodded our heads when people told us it would happen "when the time was right."

But it gnawed at me. I felt like a failure. Maybe I had done something wrong. And then those ugly voices started to whisper that maybe I'd *never* be able to have children, that I wasn't cut out to be a mother, or that I'd been too hard on my body over the years. We hadn't been trying to get pregnant, but now . . . things were changing.

The first time I saw Scott Duke, I knew I was going to marry him. It was spring of my sophomore year in college, and way down deep, I knew it. He was playing first base in an intramural softball game at Wofford College, and I had come with the pitcher. I kept trying to smile at the guy I came with, but I could barely take my eyes off this tall, dark, and gorgeous guy wearing the Duke baseball cap at first base. I left without knowing his name, and the guy I came to the game with and I dated for a year before we eventually split up the following spring. He was a great guy, but we were both made for someone else.

My junior year had been hard, so when a friend invited me to a meeting of the Fellowship of Christian Athletes on a Wednesday that spring, I said yes because I needed a change of direction, a fresh start. I attended Converse College, an all-women's school, and we didn't have an FCA chapter on campus, so the kind student-athletes at Wofford College, about a mile and a half down the road, extended an open invitation for Converse students to join their FCA meetings. I doubt the Wofford ladies appreciated our attendance, but any chance to mingle with the male species was high on the priority list for us "Connies."

My friend and I got there just as the meeting was starting. Some guy made some announcements and I looked around and stopped breathing as I made eye contact with *the first baseman from the intramural game.* He flashed a spectacular smile at me that made my knees go weak. I'm not kidding; I felt like I was in a Judy Blume novel. The guy was still saying words up front while I tried to act cool, and he explained the "mingler" we were about to start. I vaguely understood that everybody was supposed to take off one shoe and throw it into a big pile, and then each person would pick a shoe and find its owner to pray for them.

I wasn't really interested in praying, but I laser-focused my sights on the shoe First Base was untying, and, I swear, when the announcement guy said *Go!* I elbowed two people and dove over a row of girls to grab that size-13 Adidas cross-trainer. I had to crawl out of the pile of shoes, and then I feigned that I didn't know who the shoe belonged to, walking around near First Base, asking whose shoe it was. I finally bumped into First Base, and he said, "Um, I think that's mine."

"Really?" (It's all very embarrassing.)

I don't remember any praying going on that night. I mostly tried to act all coy and cool, even with half of my hair hanging out of my ponytail from the shoe pile dive. He noticed my basketball keychain, and we realized we both played on our college basketball teams. *My gosh, this is destiny.* I remembered something about him having exams he needed to do well on, so later that week, I mailed a note to his campus post office box telling him I'd be praying for him during his exams. I forgot about the praying part, but I did leave my number at the bottom of the note.

He called me two days later. We both bombed our exams that spring after spending our first two unofficial dates studying together in the library.

In the summer, I rode jet-skis with him at Lake Murray on weekends, and he came to visit me at the camp for special needs children where I worked as a lifeguard and counselor. We wrote letters to each other every week. He was the one, and we both knew it.

When school started back, we were official, and I came to every FCA meeting since he'd been elected president in the spring. One night after an FCA gathering, I was pouting in the passenger seat as he drove me home.

"What's wrong?"

"Nothing."

Silence.

"Okay, nothing's wrong?"

"No . . ."

More silence.

"Okay, I don't know what's wrong if you don't tell me."

Big sigh. "I just don't get why you don't spend any time with me at FCA. You talk to everybody else and ignore me the whole time. I'm just going to stop coming if you're going to ignore me . . ."

He pulled the car over into an empty parking lot, put it in park, and turned and looked me square in the eye.

"Listen, Wendy, I really like you. I like where this is going. But you need to know that God's called me to ministry. My job—my calling— is to minister to people, to serve people, to help people. I already know you know God because you've told me, but those people who come on Wednesday nights, they need God, and it's my responsibility to point them to Him. I can spend time with you afterwards, but in there, I have a responsibility. I'm telling you this upfront, because if you're not okay with that, maybe we aren't supposed to be together."

That is not how I thought that conversation would go. I was kind of expecting him to apologize and promise he'd show me more attention next time. So I just sat there, stunned, scraping my pride out of the floorboard. And then pride kicked in.

Whaaaattttt? Did he just totally blow me off? I do not have to take this . . .

He drove me to my dorm, and I got out and told him I'd have to think about that.

And I did. All night. I lay there thinking about how this was unlike any relationship I'd ever been in, how this guy knew what his life was about and it wasn't wrapped up in me. That took a lot of pressure off, in a weird way. Though I knew he cared about me, I wasn't the center of his world. His life was built on something solid; it didn't rise or fall on our relationship or any other circumstance. And that was something I wanted.

So I did something I hadn't done much before. I swallowed my pride, and I apologized. Though I said something like *I can deal with your responsibilities on Wednesdays,* what I meant was that I wanted to be part of a bigger plan too. I wanted my life to be centered on something strong and solid, too. I wanted to be with someone whose life was about more than him, and about more than me.

I knew what I was signing up for.

And it was this strength, this having his life wrapped around something solid, that got us through those first few years of marriage.

My spirit wouldn't have survived without this young man in a baseball cap who knew who he was and Who we belonged to.

Because our life was about to go sideways.

The second miscarriage was, by far, the most devastating. It took us a year to work up the courage to try again, even though I thought about it every day. I mourned in the secrecy of my bathroom every month. And when I skipped a cycle in February, we rushed to the obstetrician's office where the blood test was positive. I acted like we'd won the lottery. My mother kept saying, "Don't get your hopes up yet," which I took as a personal affront, though it wasn't meant to be. It was very early, but I made this pregnancy my mission. I would not fail this time.

We were about eight weeks along. Everything was looking great when I started having some mild cramping and spotting. A frantic trip to the doctor set my mind temporarily at ease when the ultrasound showed a tiny heartbeat (the first I'd ever seen), and the doctor reassured me that my symptoms were perfectly normal. They even sent me back to work with a little black-and-white photo of a white blip next to a white spot: a cryptic snapshot of a heartbeat that lit up the page and inflated my hope. I carried that photo everywhere, like a promise in my pocket.

But the cramping and bleeding escalated over the next few days, and I was sitting in the bleachers at a tournament watching our junior varsity girls play when I knew for sure where this was heading. I called Scott to come pick me up, and we eventually spent a long, agonizing Saturday afternoon trying to prevent what was already done and praying for a miracle.

Our sweet dream turned into a sweaty nightmare that ended with a flush on a Saturday night in our little pink bathroom. For hours I lay in my own personal hell with my knees curled up to my chest to try to ease the pain, crying out to my husband, "God *cannot* do this to us again! I won't forgive Him this time. I cannot forgive Him for this!"

My sweet husband had no idea what to do; he was twenty-five years old and postponing his own grief to hold us together. He just sat on his side of the bed, holding my hand and looking at the door to the bathroom.

Later, when the weeping and gnashing of teeth had subsided, he got up and pulled the handle on the toilet. That is a heavy burden for a man.

When I heard the toilet flush, I stopped crying. It was over. I shut down. I had hit the bottom of my shallow little world.

The third pregnancy, six months later, was the least traumatic only because we hadn't set our hearts on it yet. I remembered not to "get my hopes up." This became my mantra. I bound up any fledgling hope like the foot of an ancient Chinese girl, breaking its bones and distorting it into something small and controlled. But that is not hope. Hope is light and feathery, like Emily Dickinson said. Hope, unrestrained, rises up with big, gusty wings and helps us carry our burdens. My fear of hope was ripping the wings off of our marriage. The unspoken weight of not being able to have a baby was heavy on both of us. It covered everything like a wet blanket. I had taken the pregnancy test on a Thursday and had not yet even told Scott that it was positive because I was chaperoning a retreat in the mountains with some high school students, and didn't want to—(sigh)—get his hopes up. We were also negotiating a contract on a house I'd set my sights on, and I was relieved to have a break from the stress we'd been under, so I just decided to wait and tell him when I got home. So when the cramping and bleeding began that Saturday morning, I was the only one who knew what we were losing.

Nonetheless, it broke my heart. I finally called Scott, who came and picked me up and took me to lunch overlooking the Blue Ridge Mountains. We drank sweet tea and promised each other we'd keep no secrets and spare each other no heartache. We were in this together. Our heartaches should be shared too. They belonged to both of us.

So here we were again. Eight months after the last miscarriage, four years after we were first married, we sat in yet another waiting room, listening for our last name to be called from behind a plexiglass window. We were both trying not to think about how many times we'd been here—well, not *here* exactly, but in a room like this one. We were trying desperately to write a different ending.

Scott's leg danced. I kept touching his knee with my hand to make him stop. He checked his watch again as I searched my fingernails for something to chew on and looked around the empty lobby for another magazine to flip through.

"What time was our appointment, again?" he asked.

"Three o'clock," I answered.

"Well, it's three-thirty."

"Okay, why don't you—oooh!" I grabbed Scott's hand and placed it on my plump belly. "Can you *feel* that?!"

He looked at the spot where his hand rested, eyes squinted in concentration as he tried hard to detect movement underneath. He looked back to me, smiling and shaking his head with apology.

"I don't feel anything."

Just then the baby placed a ninja kick right under his palm.

"Oh my *good*-ness," he burst. "Was *that* the *baby*?!!"

"Duke!" The receptionist interrupted our moment. Scott pulled me to my feet and, smiling, we walked toward the sliding glass window at the desk. She pointed and said, "Go through that doorway, then turn right, and someone will be waiting for you at the last door on the right."

We followed her directions and were met by a perky technician who introduced herself as Paula and walked us inside. She helped me up into a black vinyl lounge chair and said, "Daddy, you can sit right there beside her," pointing to a seat at my left. Paula explained the procedure as she turned down the lights and began to squeeze lime green gel onto a hand-held roller.

"This is going to be a little bit cold," she warned. She turned the metal instrument over and began rolling it over my belly. A big glob slid down the curve of my abdomen and oozed into the elastic waistband of my maternity jeans.

We turned our eyes to the top left corner of the room where a large television monitor was mounted to the ceiling. As she maneuvered the probe over my midsection, we could see whirs of gray, white, and black blobs on the screen, unrecognizable until Paula began pointing out tiny body parts.

"There's baby's head . . . here's the backbone . . . see baby's little foot?" I could hear in her voice that she loved her job. She asked if we had picked out names, and she talked to the baby as if it could hear her, speaking in that sing-songy voice we use with babies. "Hey there, cutie. Show us your face. Turn around here so I can take a picture of you for your mommy and daddy."

I glanced over to catch Scott's reaction. He looked like a little kid on Christmas morning, an expression of pure wonder on his face. We sat holding hands and gazing at this long-awaited baby for the first time. Finally, Paula asked what we then thought was The Most Important Question.

"Would you like to know if baby is a boy or a girl?"

I turned again to my husband, the die-hard traditionalist, to see if maybe he had changed his mind. He smirked back at me.

"Go ahead. Wendy thinks she already knows it's a girl anyway. Just tell us."

Paula moved the roller around a little, saying, "I've already seen what I need to know. Can you tell yet?" We both leaned up and squinted at the screen, still only seeing variations of black and white.

"I'm assuming if you can tell that easily, it must be a boy," Scott guessed.

"Actually, it's much easier to tell for sure when it's a girl. Girls have a pelvic bone that boys don't have. It's unmistakable on a sonogram like this—see these two white lines?"

"So it *is* a girl?!" I said.

Paula smiled and nodded. "Baby is a girl," she announced.

Scott pulled my hand to his face and kissed it. "We have a daughter," he whispered.

Over the next ten or fifteen minutes, Paula took measurements and made notes on the computer screen while we watched the monitor and made our own comments: "Look! Is that her face?! Can you tell how much she weighs? There's a hand!" Paula took picture after picture for us to take home. She seemed more serious now, so we tried not to ask all the giddy new-parent questions so that she could do her job.

Suddenly, she said, "Could you both hold up your left hand for me, please?" Scott and I looked at each other quizzically, and we raised our hands up for her to see. "Hmm," then a second later, "Baby's left pinky finger is crooked. I just wanted to see if maybe she inherited it from one of you, but I guess she didn't."

"You mean like this?" Scott looked up from his lap and held up his other hand.

Paula smiled and nodded. "Baby has Daddy's hands."

I had never noticed the curve in Scott's right pinky finger before, but I don't think I've ever seen him look so proud. His eyes glistened again as he looked back at his hand for a moment, then lowered it slowly and turned back to the monitor. My husband is a big man, but this little girl had already wrapped him around her tiny, crooked little finger.

Paula seemed, for some reason, to be relieved.

She was quiet as she finished taking measurements and told us to *wait right here*, she would be *right back*: she needed to let the doctor know we were finished and he could come in. When she left the room, Scott and I began placing all of our dreams into the *Girl* category: what her name would be, pink or yellow for the nursery, little dresses and dolls. As Scott talked about our daughter and her future for the first time, it dawned on me that this was finally real to him. My body had sung—and sometimes screamed—the reality of this baby every day for the last four months, but today was his first real encounter with our child. I was seriously loving him more with every word that came out of his mouth. But as he continued to talk, a dark thought crept up on the periphery, and I suddenly remembered that we were *waiting*—waiting for another doctor to come and look at another ultrasound screen—and my chest started to tighten. Fear began its rise.

"What's the matter?" Scott asked.

"Something's not right," I said. "I think something's wrong with the baby."

"Why in the world would you think that?"

"I don't know. I just have a bad feeling. Something about Paula's demeanor changed before she left. It makes me think she saw something abnormal."

"She would have told us if something was wrong, don't you think?"

"I don't know. I guess so. Maybe I'm just being paranoid."

Finally, Paula came back in and said, "The doctor is in a meeting right now, but he'll be right in to go over everything with you. Is there anything else you'd like to look at while we have a few extra minutes?" She began to roll over my stomach again. But I noticed that she wasn't saying much, and she hadn't made eye contact since she came back in. I looked over at her face. Her eyebrows were drawn together and she squinted— like she was looking *for* something. Waves of hot fear began to wash over my chest and shoulders, and my heart was thumping in my throat. Finally, I couldn't wait anymore.

"Paula, is something wrong?"

This girl had only known us for about forty-five minutes. But her eyes filled with tears, and she said, "I don't know how to tell you this, but—" Her voice broke. "Baby has only one leg."

The air disappeared, and my whole life shifted with that one sentence. As Paula began to cry openly and apologize for being so emotional all at the same time, Scott and I just sat and blinked at her. We had been holding hands since we sat down, but now we each instinctively held on with both hands, our fingers intertwined and knuckles white. For some odd reason, I kept trying to console Paula.

"It's okay—we're okay, I promise," I said to her over and over, but I don't know why now. She was wiping her eyes and trying to show us pictures of our baby's legs. She showed us both legs and took measurements of each again. The left leg was about a quarter of the length of the right leg with no foot or knee.

Paula was losing it. "I am so sorry," she sobbed. "Excuse me, please. I'm going to go tell the doctor to get in here *right now*." When she shut the door behind her, we just sat for a few minutes of stunned silence. I blinked in slow motion and turned to look at my husband; he leaned over and laid his cheek on our tangled hands. His face crumpled, and we both started to cry.

I don't know why we cared about keeping ourselves pulled together, but we did, and by the time Paula came back with the doctor, we had dried our eyes and were waiting for some kind of explanation.

The doctor finally came in, introduced himself, shook hands with Scott, and then quickly sent Paula to go clean herself up. He looked at the measurements Paula had taken, and then checked the baby again so he could see for himself. He was mumbling something about statistics and how often something like this happens and what the possible causes could be, but I wasn't listening. I was looking at my baby's third ultrasound and thinking about what her life would be like with one leg. And I started to plead silently.

"Please, God, please let this be a mistake. Let Paula have been wrong. Please. *Please.*"

But she wasn't wrong. The doctor confirmed the measurements Paula had taken and asked us to follow him to his office where he walked behind his desk and sat down. There was one chair facing his desk and an upholstered high-back in the corner that Scott picked up and started to place next to me.

"Please don't move my furniture," the doctor said without looking up. I honestly thought the man must have been kidding. But Scott set the chair back in place and stood beside me while this doctor told us all the possible causes of the "underdeveloped limb." We listened to every detail, searching for the one that gave us some hope that the leg could still grow. He told us it could be a blood clot that restricted blood supply to the leg; it could be something called amniotic bands that could have stunted growth; it could be spina bifida or some other genetic disorder. He asked about our family histories: Scott had an older brother who died in infancy after being born with spina bifida, and our first miscarriage was the result of a genetic defect called Trisomy 18. The doctor's face changed, and he pushed back in his chair when I mentioned the Trisomy. He told us we had a much greater risk of having another child with Trisomy 18, and we needed to "consider all of our options."

He then led us to a small room with a television and brought in a video illustrating how an amniocentesis is performed. He told us he thought we needed to have an amniocentesis in a couple of days to see if the problem was genetic. Then he said, "If this is Trisomy 18, you really need to consider your options and make some informed choices. Trisomy babies are severely deformed, and they don't live very long *if* they survive childbirth." He told us that "terminating the pregnancy" might be the most "reasonable" decision for us. He reminded us that we were young and would have other chances to have children. Then he closed the door and left us alone to watch the video.

I don't remember anything about that video. Those fifteen minutes were a darkening whirlwind of our voices talking together, protesting together, agreeing together.

When the doctor came back in, Scott stood and helped me up and said, "We'll have the amnio done because we want to be as prepared for this baby as we possibly can. But we want you to know right now that there is no 'option' for us. Whatever we find out, we'll put it in God's hands."

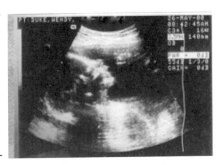

Ultrasound at 21 weeks

The doctor tried to urge again, "But you don't understand how bad this could—"

"No, *you* don't understand."

Scott spoke up for the three of us, guiding me on wobbly legs toward the door. "This choice is not ours to make. She's not *just* ours. She belongs to God."

We left him looking at us and scheduled an amniocentesis for the following week.

CHAPTER 2

BEARING BAD NEWS

For you created my inmost being;

You knit me together in my mother's womb.

I will praise you because I am fearfully and wonderfully made.

Your works are wonderful; I know that full well.

My frame was not hidden from you

when I was made in the secret place.

When I was woven together in the depths of the earth,

Your eyes saw my unformed body;

All the days ordained for me were written in your book

before one of them came to be.

~ Psalm 139:13–16

WE DROVE HOME FROM THE doctor's office almost in silence. We had already arranged to meet my family at Rock-o-la Diner for dinner that evening to let them know the gender of the baby. They were all waiting at a booth when we arrived. My mom, dad, and youngest sister all sat with sly grins on their faces. My middle sister, Heather, was at a work seminar in Nashville, Tennessee, but this couldn't wait until she got home. I had played this scene out fifty times since we left the office, trying to figure out exactly how to tell them, but when I saw their excited faces, I panicked. I just couldn't do it yet.

We showed them the sonogram pictures, and they *ooohed* and *ah-hhed* at the face, the hands, the clearly defined right foot. Then my sister Jenny said, "Well, are you gonna tell us? Is it a girl or a boy?"

Scott and I looked at each other. "It's a girl," I said, swallowing hard. "But we need to tell you something else."

"It's twins!" my daddy guessed.

By this time, I couldn't look at them. I just shook my head.

"No, sir," I choked out and took a deep breath to recover. "She has only one leg."

I try to imagine how I would respond if somebody blurted that news at me, especially someone in my family. I guess I was expecting some sort of emotional breakdown that I just knew would send me over the edge. But my sweet family handled it like champions. My mama immediately sat up tall, raised her chin, and said, "Okay, there are a lot of things she can do with just one leg. There are lots of sports and activities for children with disabilities. You two will be the perfect parents for her."

I've never needed my mother to be as strong as I needed her to be in that moment. She was amazing. Now that I am a mother, I understand what she must have been feeling. And I'm sure she had her own emotional breakdown later on. But in those first overwhelming moments, God had anointed her with strength, composure, and wisdom that kept me from plummeting into the deep pit of despair where I was teetering at the edge. I've never needed as much encouragement as I needed sitting in that red vinyl booth that evening, and my family was flawless. My sweet baby sister Jenny was all smiles and positive words, although I know her heart was broken for me. And my daddy's calm strength needed few words to communicate what I needed to know: that God had placed this little girl into an amazing family full of love and support and encouragement that would equip her to fulfill the plans He had for her life.

I can't leave out my middle sister, Heather, who called us later that night from out of town. I was sitting in our big red chair when she called, and I asked her if she was in a place where she could talk in private. She was visiting one of our childhood friends, the brother of one of my closest friends who was due with her first child any day. I didn't want Jud to tell Caroline about this before I did. So Heather went into another room, and I told her about the ultrasound. She was so sweet even though I could tell she was trying not to cry. Heather's not big on drama or sentimentality. She just said, "I know everything's gonna be okay. I love you." And that was enough.

That night, Scott and I lay in bed and cried. I cried, and I cried, and I cried. Scott wrapped me up in his arms until I was too tired to cry anymore. We just lay there, looking at the ceiling, for a long time. And then we decided on her name.

Since our first pregnancy, we had always loved the name Savannah. Scott's parents grew up in the beautiful city in Georgia, and we had driven there countless times to see grandmothers, aunts, uncles, and cousins. It was our favorite getaway place for spring break trips with college friends and summer road trips. It was in Savannah, the year after we met in college, that our marriage was first prophesied by his cousin, David. After the three of us had spent about four hours playing pick-up basketball games until the courts closed at dark, I asked,

"Can we not find another court that has lights?" David pulled the car over to the side of Victory Drive, turned to Scott from behind the steering wheel, and said, "You have got to *marry* this girl!"

Besides the frequent visits, my all-time favorite book was *The Prince of Tides*, whose beloved heroine was a young girl who shared her name with the great southern city. In the Civil War, Savannah had been spared being burned to the ground by the dreaded General Sherman when the mayor and townspeople met his troops outside the gates of the city and offered the town's resources. We wanted her to have a name that conjured beauty, strength, and resilience. So we made up our minds early that Savannah would be our baby's first name.

But we had never decided on a middle name. For some reason, lying quietly in bed late that night, Grace was the only name we could think of. We pulled out a dictionary to research its meaning:

grace [n] 1. *charm, loveliness, elegance*

2. *mercy, unmerited favor, pardon*

It seemed like the only word we could place right in the center of this little girl of ours. So it was decided: Savannah Grace Duke. We got down on our knees on the side of the bed, and we prayed for her by name. Scott prayed long and hard, a man who believes every word he releases heavenward. But I was struggling to talk to God.

The truth was that I had more doubts than I had faith. What was going on here, anyway? Hadn't I always tried to live for the Lord—follow His ways, serve in the church, be a good influence? For what? Was this some kind of big test? If that was true, I didn't want to play anymore. Suffice it to say that the faith I had built my life on (and honestly, had prided myself in) was beginning to crumble beneath me. I had never had to flesh out this flimsy faith I'd claimed. It had no meat, no muscles, no substance. I just kept asking, *What kind of God would let this happen?* For the first time in my very sheltered life, God wasn't making my paths straight. I wasn't sure if He was really even there.

When Scott finished praying, we lay back down on the bed and looked up at the ceiling, and then we made a decision. In the dark hours of the night, we committed that we would only talk about the things she *could* do. We didn't want to dwell on all the things she wouldn't be capable of doing. We were going to have to decide to focus on what she *would be able* to do with one leg—the possibilities rather than the obstacles. We named out loud all the things she'd be able to do: piano, art, singing, hopscotch, writing, reading, medicine, science, graphic arts . . .

We fell asleep dreaming possibilities for her future.

That first week was a long one. I went to school the next day after the ultrasound and stumbled through the motions of teaching three ninety-minute English classes until the end of the day. Then I sat down in our athletic director's office and unraveled. Deb Osborne had called me a few weeks after my first miscarriage two years earlier and offered me my first head coaching job. She had been through the last two miscarriages with me since I came on staff. We talked about how this would affect next season, and although it was her job to look out for the athletic program, she never once entertained my offer to resign for the sake of the team. She said we'd do whatever we needed to do. Deb is as tough as anybody I know, but that day she was a loyal, compassionate friend and a great listener. And I needed both.

That afternoon, Scott and I drove to Columbia and met Scott's parents for an early dinner. As soon as the waitress took our drink orders, Scott's mom said, "Okay, I can't wait anymore. I got a little gift for the baby, but you have to tell us if it's a boy or a girl first. I have one for a boy and one for a girl!" She handed me two small gift bags—one pink and one blue.

"Well," Scott began. "There's something we need to tell you first—"

"I knew it. It's twins, isn't it?" Scott's dad said.

Sigh. "No, it's not twins—" Scott said.

"We're having a girl," I quietly interrupted, and I handed them the sonogram pictures.

They took the black-and-white photo and acted, like everybody else, like they knew what they were looking at, cooing and gently fingering the white evidences of life.

"What else?" Scott's mom was studying the expression on Scott's face. "Is there something else?"

We hadn't choreographed this, and we both looked at each other to see who would speak first. My voice was lodged in my throat. I couldn't do it.

"She has one leg," Scott said.

I wish I could remember more about the rest of the conversation. The truth is that I was emotionally spent by that time; the rest was just a blur of questions and limited answers. The best I can describe these talks (and there would be more) is that people just respond with reserved shock. Nobody wants to cry or ask the deeper questions we all had. Really, what could you say to two young parents with this kind of crisis? What would *I* say? I shudder to think how I would respond, because I am horrifically awkward in dealing with others' crises and loss. I am forever sticking my foot in my mouth and stumbling for appropriate words that *do not come out the way I want them to.*

Our families handled it much better than I would have. They didn't feel the need to fill the void with words. Just love.

But I do remember the end of the dinner. Our plates had hardly been touched. We told them her name: Savannah Grace. And then Scott suggested I open the pink gift bag.

"Um, let's wait until later," his mom said, trying to scoop both gift bags off the table.

"Please. I need something happy right now," I said and began to pull out the pink tissue paper. I lifted a small box from inside the bag and opened the lid.

Inside was a tiny pair of black, patent-leather Mary Jane shoes. We all began to cry.

I really thought I'd be okay after that. I had made it through a school day, told both of our families, and didn't think I had any tears left to cry. But grief doesn't work like that; it doesn't follow any rules. It comes flying out of the bushes and throws itself down on top of you just when you think you've tamed it. Wednesday morning, standing in front of the bathroom mirror, wielding a hair dryer and roller brush at 7 a.m., I fell apart. Just sat down on the lid of the toilet seat and wept until I slid to a heap on the floor and threw up. I couldn't pull myself up off the floor and couldn't bear the thought of trying to convince a roomful of carefree teenagers to appreciate *The Crucible.* My sweet husband called the school for me, and then talked to Deb and asked if she or the guidance counselor could explain the situation to my students. He took the day off with me. We just sat in our house and didn't try to convince ourselves that we were okay.

The rest of the week was a countdown to the amniocentesis appointment. We met with our friends Brian and Carrie on Friday night to let them know what was going on before Sunday. Brian was a teacher in our Bible study class, and we wanted them to know the situation just in case neither of us could make it through telling our friends at church and asking for the kind of prayer we needed.

On Sunday, during the time for prayer requests, my heart was thumping in my neck by the time I raised my hand. I don't think I said four words before I choked up and turned to Scott for help. But he wouldn't look at me. I realized that he too was trying not to weep openly, so I swallowed hard and told the class about our ultrasound results. I could hear people sniffling all around the room, although I couldn't see anybody through my tears.

I will never forget the next few minutes. I'm sure that some-body had prepared a great Bible lesson for that day, but our whole class got up and circled around us and prayed out loud for us and for Savannah. I specifically remember my friend Deidre reminding God of His promises for a hope and future for our little girl and rebuking the possibility that there was a chromosomal disorder or any other medical problem with the baby that would threaten her life. She spoke life-giving promises over the next day's appointment—that there would be no trace of Trisomy 18 and that we would be empow-ered by what we saw at the amniocentesis. She'll never know what those words did for me.

Because I have to tell you the truth, the darkest secret I've ever kept: I thought a lot about what that doctor said. I had lain in bed with his words echoing in my mind. *You really need to consider your options . . . babies like this don't live long . . . you don't know how bad this could be . . .*

And I have to tell you that during those long nights after Scott had fallen asleep, the one thing I never thought I could even *consider* considering was lurking in the dark shadows of my thoughts. There was no question that we would protect our baby at all costs, but for the first time, I could empathize with the despair of a girl sitting in her car outside of a clinic, scared, confused, not thinking straight. Anguishing over what life will be like. Not seeing any resolution. Grieving over shattered dreams and Camelot lost. Just wishing it could all be like it was before. Hearing the voices banging around in her head: *You're young . . . don't ruin your life . . . you need to consider your options . . .*

Those voices are loud. They're deafening if they're the only ones in your ear. We need others' voices to shout them down, scream into the abyss, *Enough! You just shut up!*

Sometimes the decibels of hurt make even the strongest of us lose our minds, all semblance of reason and clear thinking disabled. This is why God reminds us not to stop meeting together, encouraging each other, speaking truth into each other's lives: to tell us we are not alone in this.

This is how my friends, on that Sunday morning, silenced those hissing, murmuring whispers following me around in the darkness. This is how they spoke life into me instead. They reminded me of truth.

Scott and I wept that day as our brothers and sisters placed their hands on us and claimed God's promises for our daughter and for us as her parents. It was a monumental morning for us, there in the comfort of our church home where the spiritually sick, wounded, and weary come for relief and help. Their words were weighty enough to help us through the grueling battle we were about to face.

Careless words stab like a sword,
but the words of wise people bring healing.
~ Proverbs 12:18 (GW)

Speak up for those who cannot speak for themselves,
for the rights of all who are destitute.
~ Proverbs 31:8

CHAPTER 3

PREPARING FOR BATTLE

For I know the plans I have for you," declares the Lord,
"plans to prosper you and not to bring you harm, plans to give
you hope and a future."

~ Jeremiah 29:11

EIGHT DAYS AFTER THAT FIRST ultrasound, we returned to the same doctor's office for an amniocentesis. Dr. No-Bedside-Manner (the name we had bestowed on him, among others that I will not mention) was in a more compassionate mood that day and not so concerned with the placement of his furniture. We walked back to the same room where we had seen Savannah for the first time the week before. This time though, there was a much more sober mood in the room—a cloud of heaviness hung over our heads. For one thing, I have a needle phobia and was trying not to FREAK OUT. I passed out the last time I had blood drawn, and they were about to push a six-inch-long needle into my belly *where my baby lived.*

I was trying hard to listen to the doctor's explanation of the procedure above my own heartbeat thumping in my ears. The nurse turned on the TV screen on the wall where we had watched our baby squirm last week, and then she set up and prepared my belly for another sonogram. Dr. NBM explained how he would use the sonogram with the monitor to guide the needle away from the baby. Scott asked if there was a risk of hurting her with the needle. Without looking up, the doctor said that "fetuses" usually sense the needle and try to move away from it—he said it was really quite fascinating how they instinctively sensed danger.

I thought I was going to faint. I knew this procedure was important, but I was hoping for some kind of spiritual, out-of-body experience while the needle was in there. Instead, I held Scott's hand so tightly he winced, and I closed my eyes and tried the breathing techniques I had seen in childbirth videos. I just ended up holding my breath. Finally, the needle was in. Unfortunately, I was still conscious. Though I wished I was in a medically-induced coma, I was about to see the most amazing sight I had ever before or since witnessed.

Scott told me to open my eyes, and I saw our baby on the monitor, sucking her thumb. At first, she did exactly what the doctor said she would do and moved away from the long, pointed invader of her space. But then we squinted our eyes and leaned in closer as, slowly but surely, her tiny hand reached out and blew our minds.

She grabbed the shaft of the needle.

I was afraid to move, but Scott shot to his feet. "Did she—? Is that—?"

The doctor froze and stared at the monitor too. "The baby seems to be, ah, holding the instrument. I've heard of this happening before, but I've, ah, never actually seen it." He finished drawing out the fluid and eased the shaft of the needle out of the tiny fingers that held it hostage. I could have sworn Savannah shook her fist at him.

We all just sat there with our mouths hanging open. Scott and I turned to look at each other, and at the same time, we both said, "Did that just happen?!"

The amnio results were inconclusive. The doctor still had no explanation for the "limb defect" and couldn't definitively rule out spina bifida, though the amniotic fluid tested negatively for Trisomy 18. He explained to us that the leg would not grow—the stage of development where the legs and arms are formed had long passed. He squelched any hope that the left leg could miraculously catch up with the right. Again, he reminded us that we still had a "choice"—that he did not want us to feel pressured or forced into continuing the pregnancy knowing that limb deficiencies often coincided with other birth defects. He dangled *Choice* before us like a proverbial carrot.

But I had done my homework. I'd had some dark and sleepless nights over the prior week, moments of fear and confusion and vulnerability. Moments where I heard the doctor's words ringing in my ears: *possible brain abnormality . . . marital and financial stress . . . suffering after birth.* So I researched these *options*; I dug to find out exactly what the procedures entailed. I saw and read what doctors did to fetuses when they terminated pregnancies.

One horrifying glimpse at the violent measures taken to end a pregnancy at twenty weeks brought all my doubts to a screeching halt. I wept over what I saw medical professionals do to these babies.

I had *seen* my baby kicking and sucking her thumb and reaching for the needle, responding to a foreign object with both fear and curiosity. I could not reconcile those images with the ones I saw on the computer screen before me, the violence inflicted on a *human being that is already responsive to its surroundings.* Our doctor did not explain this procedure; he did not inform us of this kind of carnage or suffering. I could not fathom how this would bring healing of any kind.

No. This was not a choice I was entitled to. A thousand times no.

If the doctor told us anything else or was even in the room after Savannah grabbed the needle, we didn't notice. Something happened to us in that moment in the sonogram room. We walked out with a sense of empowerment—a spirit of courage and power that comes from seeing someone rise up against an enemy. We drove home with a war cry ringing in our ears, a rebel yell to gear up and battle hard against whatever this enemy was that stood in front of us. We had ourselves a fighter.

We actually thought about changing her name to Xena (you know, the warrior princess from the late 90s TV show) but decided that might be *a little* over the top. She'd have enough to deal with on the first day of school.

In a profound way, that doctor's appointment changed us. We were strengthened and flat-out *inspired* by this little daughter of ours who hadn't yet been born: a twenty-one-week-old fetus that the medical profession doesn't yet consider to be a person. She called out the warriors in us that day. We got ready for battle.

Over the next few months leading up to Savannah's birth, we began to prepare ourselves physically, emotionally, and spiritually.

We painted and filled the baby's room with new baby shower gifts and accessories, and Scott brought home no less than a gazillion stuffed animals for her from a mission trip to China. I decided to go with a Noah's ark theme since he had smuggled in every species of stuffed animal on the planet. Like every expectant parent, we registered for the necessary items at Babies R Us and stocked her room with Pampers and baby wipes. We were given a book called *Giraffes Can't Dance,* a sweet little rhyming story that Scott read to her through my belly-button every night. The hero is a giraffe named Gerald who is the only animal in the jungle who can't dance, but he finally finds his groove when he hears the right music. It was a perfect story for her to hear every night. By the time she was born, Scott could recite the whole story without opening the book. *Sometimes when you're different, you just need a different song . . .*

That summer, Scott and I went on a trip to China with some teachers. I was seven months pregnant by then, and because the Chinese government only allows couples to have one child, pregnant women are a rarity and a *very big deal.* Everybody treated me like a queen, which—I'm not gonna lie—was kind of awesome. I got to sit on a sofa all day long and sip fruit smoothies while Scott and the rest of the group taught English and PE. They even made Scott carry my purse. And that was *very* awesome.

I met and became friends with a lady who went by the English name "Annie." One night, as we were walking to dinner, Annie began to ask me questions about my baby. Honestly, I don't even know how or why I brought it up, but I told her that the baby only had one leg. We were walking up a flight of steps, and I realized Annie had stopped on the bottom step. I turned around to check on her, and she was just standing there looking at the ground.

"Annie, are you okay?"

She hesitated and kept her eyes on the ground before saying, in broken English, "Mrs. Wendy, I hope my question is not rude. But why are you having this baby this way? Why do you not stop this pregnancy and have another baby again? Have a healthy baby next time?"

I stared at her for a second, struggling to keep my emotions reigned in. And then I remembered the book I'd read on the plane about Chinese families. In China, it said, you get one chance to have a baby, and if anything about that baby is less than perfect, abortion is the logical choice. According to the accounts, babies are aborted for being girls, for having birth defects or Down's syndrome, or sometimes just for being the second child, as second births are against the law. I sat down on the step where I stood and took a deep breath.

"Annie, my husband and I believe in God. We believe God created people—every person—and that he has a plan and a purpose for every life that he creates. We believe he has a plan for this baby. And we believe it would be wrong for us to take away life that God created."

We just sat and looked at each other for a minute. I wondered if she understood a word I'd said.

Then she said, "Your God, does he have a name?"

And I smiled at her. "Jesus," I said. "His name is Jesus." And I began to tell her, as simply as I could, how God became man, and was placed inside of Mary, and how she carried the baby Jesus even though people said her pregnancy was wrong. I told her the story of how Jesus was born and how the angels invited the shepherds to come see him first, and how wise men heard about him and came from far away to see him and how he loved us all and lived a perfect life so that we could follow it and how he sacrificed his life so that we could have freedom.

I looked up at her, and I kind of laughed a little. "Does this sound a little crazy?"

But she shook her head. "Maybe not crazy. Maybe I feel a little hope. Like maybe life is not hopeless."

Every night that summer, we prayed. Scott laid his face on my ever-swelling belly and pleaded to our baby's Creator. We prayed for her health, for our readiness as parents, for acceptance of God's will. We were even part of a couple of prayer services specifically held for healing. But I gradually began to realize that Scott's expectations and mine were not the same.

There is a vast difference between *deliverance* and *delivery*. Deliverance is what Scott asked for: relief, escape, being freed from harm or hurt. We researched and read stories about how God had granted deliverance of his people from slavery, from plagues, illnesses, even from death. Scott held onto to these verses from Scripture like tickets to be redeemed. He believed that God would heal her. He believed she would be born with two perfect legs and was already looking forward to the opportunity to tell everybody who would listen how God had miraculously healed his little girl. Because he knew God could do it.

I love him for this.

But sometimes God chooses a less direct path. Sometimes He guides us along twisted, high roads that lead us to places we would have never seen if we'd taken the marked route. As the weeks and months went by, I had the distinct sense God was whispering something different to my spirit. In a hushed, gentle breath, God spoke: *This is who I created her to be. This is who she is. This is what I have prepared you for.*

I tried to pretend I didn't hear it. This wasn't supposed to happen. We were supposed to raise a team of tiny basketball players, just like we'd always planned. Ten fingers and toes and all that. We had this all planned out: three little mini-Scott-and-Wendy clones who could shoot a jump shot and run like the wind and dribble through their legs—

My ways are higher than your ways.

I tried not to listen. But my mind began returning to the summers I had spent working at Camp Burnt Gin, a camp specifically for disabled and special needs children. Those were some of the most sacred days of my life, those sweltering months in the South Carolina low-country between college semesters where I played games and sang goofy songs and splashed in the pool and took care of children who couldn't feed themselves, couldn't walk, couldn't speak. They were the most grateful children in the whole wide world. My heart was stolen by kids who struggled every day to fit in, to be normal, to survive. And their smiles flashed into my thoughts when I thought about my unborn daughter. *Has God actually prepared me for this, primed my heart for this? Could it be that I was being equipped all those years ago?*

We continued to pray for complete healing, for a miraculous change at our next ultrasound. I ignored the still, small voice and reasoned that it was my own fears, my own doubt—lack of faith. But day after day, God quietly pressed into my heart the same words: *I have created her exactly the way I wanted her. This is who she is. This is what I have prepared you for.* Even as I begged and pleaded for a different response, in my heart of hearts, I knew this was it.

Delivery is different than deliverance. Delivery is a distribution or transfer of goods: a package, a message, a meat lover's pizza. While Scott was praying for deliverance, I got a delivery. God had delivered a clear message. There would be no deliverance. Not in the way we thought it should be.

I don't know why He chose to speak this to me and not to Scott. I never told my husband what I heard. I knew he had his hopes set on God healing her completely, and frankly, I hoped I was wrong. I hoped that somehow I had screwed up this message and that God hadn't answered at all.

I wished it had been the other way around, that God had spoken to Scott instead, because as soon as I was sure about the message, I shut down. I just stopped talking to God altogether. Oh, I still stayed involved in church, still read the Bible, still bowed my head for the blessing before every meal. I wasn't overtly defiant. After all, my whole life had become this manufactured world of God and church and faith—I was a Sunday school teacher, for cryin' out loud. I couldn't just abandon God, or more importantly, the life we'd built around Him, even if my heart wasn't in it. But I didn't want any more heart-to-hearts. Anybody who's ever been really hurt by someone they love knows this kind of disappointment and need for distance.

But it can't last too long; hurt has to be treated before it turns to something rotten.

I was just plain mad. Really, really mad. I couldn't get past the elephant constantly in the room: if He really was God, He could have changed the outcome. He could have kept it from happening altogether. But He didn't. Didn't He care about us? Didn't He know how hard this was going to be? Did He even see us? He said He had prepared me for this. *Prepared* me? I didn't feel qualified or ready for any of this. And why in the world would He *create* a disability, not give her a fighting chance at life? Life was hard enough as it was. Why did she have to start out with so much to overcome? It just didn't seem fair. These were the questions nobody was answering. Nobody else seemed to be even asking them.

So I gave God the silent treatment. Gave the Creator of the Universe the cold shoulder. Even as I write this I grieve at my immaturity and proud heart. Because even in my arrogance, even as I turned my back on God, I had the distinct sense that He was right behind me, following me around, waiting for me to talk to Him about this—pursuing me.

But I am a stubborn fool, and slow of heart sometimes, and so the last few months of my pregnancy with my firstborn were spent with a spirit of unforgiveness and a wall of bitterness between me and my God.

Not only was I hardened toward God, I was sick of people talking to me about Him. I can't count how many well-meaning people during that time told me how God could heal the baby if I believed He could, if I had faith. They sent me Scripture verses with a note telling me to "Keep the faith."

If any of you lacks wisdom, you should ask God, who gives generously to all without finding fault, and it will be given to you. But when you ask, you must believe and not doubt.

~ James 1:5–6a

Jesus replied, "Truly I tell you, if you have faith and do not doubt . . . If you believe, you will receive whatever you ask for in prayer."

~ Matthew 21:21–22

And it just made me madder. For cryin' out loud, I *knew* all the verses about belief and faith. I had probably taught them in a Sunday school lesson at some time. But there is a difference between knowing something in your head and believing it in your heart. I didn't know God yet.

We who are well versed in the truths of the Bible have a tendency to forget what it's like not to know God. Sometimes we throw Scripture at people like a striped life ring off the deck of a boat. *Just grab it and hold on. You'll be fine.* All the while, sharks are circling below, and the fear of drowning paralyzes any efforts to move toward rescue. We are quick to condense the Word of God into Flintstone-shaped nuggets containing all we need to be healthy and happy and whole.

Don't get me wrong; I love God's Word. I believe it is divine and powerful. The Bible is one of my most prized earthly possessions. But it's not God. I treasure it because it is one of the primary ways I discover who God is: His heart, His character, His passions. But God is not a pill. His Word is not a nicotine patch or a medicated bandage we can just press onto a wound to make it all better. The words on the page don't cure our cancer; only the Author can. He's not easy or fast or consolidated, but much more complex and majestic and enormous than what can be contained in the limited language of man. He is a feast, laid bare on the table, inviting us to partake, to savor, to chew until our jaws are tired. He's meant to be digested and absorbed into every cell of our being. The Bible has been, from the beginning, a conversation between the Creator and His creation—a heart-to-heart between a Father and His child. I had missed out on that relationship somewhere. Acquiring and using the words on the page has never been the goal. The goal is to *know God*—to discover the way a holy God sounds and looks and walks and loves.

I had formerly used the Bible to make a point. I often referenced tidbits of wisdom to distribute during the peaks and valleys of other people's lives (as in, *Here, this verse made me think of you today,* or, *Here, I thought this might help you with your decision*). I tossed it like a grenade into philosophical conversations, a haughty final blow.

The double-edged sword of Scripture was not meant to be a weapon, but a scalpel. It's an instrument of healing that splits the carnal from the spiritual. Scripture is the opposite of a fence we can sit on. It's a sharp blade that demands, *Choose. This is the line. Is God true or not true?*

But if we're not careful, we can resort to dropping Scripture on people from above like supplies from an aircraft over war-ravaged refugees, never getting close enough to get dirty or get hurt before moving off to the next stop where supplies are stacked and a new shipment will be loaded and unloaded. This was not Jesus' way. Jesus got down in the trenches with us and spoke to the heart of the matter. Although He obviously knew and spoke Scripture, He mostly asked people what they thought they needed and spoke simple truth into their pain. He *fulfilled* the Scripture, put arms and legs and flesh on it. God's Word has to be attached to love; otherwise, it loses its power. It's just words that sound like clanging cymbals.

God would send me people to bring the words to life, but while I waited out my pregnancy in rebellion, I was deaf to Scripture. All the Scripture given to me during that time was appropriate and relevant, but I didn't know God yet. I hadn't let Him in. So while the words of Scripture were true and now bring me much comfort, I didn't have God's presence to translate them. The words weren't penetrating the surface. They felt like a punch to the face when people tossed them at me. What I really wanted was for someone to sit down with me and say "This sucks. I don't know why this is happening, either."

But there are times when *no* mere words will bring comfort or answers. Only the presence of God brings the peace we really need. When the time is right and God wants us to hear from Him, He leans down into the caves we're hiding in and, with a firm whisper, coaxes us out to see the spectacular.

I knew, deep down to my core, what God had been prepping me to face, and I resented the implication that I could change the outcome by begging Him to change His mind. Even though I knew these were kind and wonderful people with perfect intentions and good hearts, I was sick of coming to the underlying conclusion that my *lack* of faith, lack of belief, could cause my baby to be deformed and handicapped. Sometimes our formulas just don't work. I believed. I believed God *could* do anything. I also was pretty sure that He had decided not to. But what was I supposed to do—*tell* people that? Just come out and say, *Okay, you can all stop praying now. God says "no"?*

So I just smiled and nodded my head and said, "Yes, yes. I know, I know." In the meantime, bitterness and resentment took root and, along with the baby inside me, grew a little each day.

On Sunday, September 17, 2000, my husband and I checked into Greenville Hospital to kick-start a real delivery. I was more than a week overdue, and my doctor had decided to induce labor the next morning. We spent a restless night preparing my body for labor and preparing our minds for this dreamed-of baby whose reality was right around the corner. We were scared.

The next morning began with an IV and a Pitocin drip, and the contractions started a few minutes later. *My* plan was to deliver this baby naturally, without pain medication and *definitely without an epidural.* Besides being deathly afraid of needles, my history as a finely tuned athlete (I almost laugh when I say that, because it is debatable whether or not I was *ever* finely tuned, but I was definitely out of tune by this time) and a high tolerance for pain gave me false confidence that I did not need an epidural to endure childbirth. My friend Deidre, who *says* she has no pain tolerance, had delivered her baby without any pain medication a few months earlier. So in my mind, there was no way I was coming out of that hospital with my head held high if I succumbed to anesthesia. But above all, I hate needles, so the epidural was out.

Seven hours later, my ambition to avoid an epidural was sheer ridiculousness. Besides the fact that every doctor in the hospital (and possibly the county) knew the history of this baby and *just happened* to be on the wing during the delivery, I have a tendency to throw up when I am in pain and there was nothing left in my stomach. So I was retching over the side of the bed and hyperventilating through off-the-chart contractions and progressing one centimeter every two hours, *and* a strange doctor was poking his or her head in every five minutes to see if the baby had been born. After I had yelled at everybody on the hall, including poor Scott, been reduced to dry-heaving, and had been told by my doctor that it looked like it would be *another twelve hours*, I waved the white flag of surrender. Pride does not exist inside the delivery room.

I got an epidural at 3:00 and thirty minutes later was fully dilated. I'm sure this surprises no one who knows me well, but my doctor explained that because I was *fighting* the contractions instead of allowing them to serve their purpose and move the baby, I had prolonged my own labor. That says more about my spiritual tendencies than I care to admit.

Once the epidural kicked in and my body relaxed, it took about twenty minutes for the baby to be ready to be delivered. My doctor was so sure it would take me another half day to deliver that we had to wait almost an hour for her to drive from another hospital across town. And so, with Scott, both of my sisters and his sister Stephanie, my obstetrician and about seventy-five gajillion other nurses, medical students, and doctors looking on, our daughter was born at 5:26

p.m. on Monday, September 18, 2000.

She was whisked away to be weighed and checked. I had some complications during the delivery, so Scott stayed with the baby while she was evaluated by the nurses. They finally brought her to my bed.

She was the most beautiful thing I had ever seen. When they pulled back the blankets and I saw her face, crowned with

The first time I held Savannah

a knit cap, I had that overwhelming sensation all mothers describe when they first see their newborn baby: total and complete love that eludes description. I held her and talked to her with Scott right beside me, and I noticed that he had been crying. Everyone was quiet. I finally said, "Can someone show me her leg?"

Scott turned his face away from me, and the nurse pulled back the blanket and showed me my daughter's left side. My tongue got stuck in my throat, and what came out of my mouth sounded more like a snort than the gasp it was. I was embarrassed at the sound. But the sight of her leg stole my voice.

My baby's left leg was twisted and gnarled with an open wound on the back. Everyone was very quiet, so I said the only thing I could think of. I placed my finger on her soft cheek and said, "You are beautiful, little girl of mine."

Scott was crying. I realized then how crushed he must have been that his prayers for healing had not been granted. But he nodded his head and said, "Yes, she is."

The nurse wrapped her back up and handed her to me while she explained that they would take her back to the Neonatal ICU for the doctors to examine her more closely.

"Why, is there something else wrong with her?" I wanted to know.

"We're just not sure exactly what we're dealing with," my doctor interjected as she stepped over to the side of the bed. "We need to keep her in the NICU until we figure out exactly what her diagnosis is."

"I'll go with her," Scott said. I held her and talked to her a few more minutes before they took her from my arms and let her daddy carry her to the NICU.

For the next two days, as I recovered in a room down the hall, Savannah slept in a little chrome crib in the NICU surrounded by nurses and doctors and babies struggling to live. I walked down the hall every couple of hours or so to hold her, and Scott stayed by her side most of the time. The nurses had wrapped her leg in a massive dressing of white gauze that looked like a giant cast. They taught us how to dress the wound ourselves, and Scott and I and other family

In NICU, one day old

members took turns feeding and rocking her. Nobody had asked me for the sweet little pink gowns I had brought from home, so when I went in to see her the first time, she was in this multi-colored, gender neutral onesie they had stashed in the NICU. That lasted about five seconds until I could dig out my favorites from among the baby shower gifts I'd packed.

My tailbone had cracked during the delivery, so I sat on a stack of pillows while feeding her a bottle in a rocking chair in the NICU. Machines beeped from the cribs of tiny preemies all around. Every pediatric doctor in the hospital had been in to see Savannah, and still no one knew exactly what we were dealing with. One doctor thought it was amniotic bands wrapped around the leg muscle; one doctor thought it was spina bifida; one doctor was called in to rule out any chromosomal disorders.

After a series of CT scans, an MRI, and a bone scan, the hospital's chief pediatric surgeon gave us the most definitive answer we had heard. "Our best diagnosis is that she suffers from a lack of a diagnosis."

On Wednesday night, I had to check out of the hospital room we had been living in for two days. There was no place for parents to stay in the NICU. It was September 20, my birthday, and I was packing up to leave for home without my baby. The results from the MRI that day were not back yet, and so they wanted to keep Savannah there until they had ruled out all the critical possibilities. They were looking for markers of spina bifida. At 10 p.m. on the night I had to leave the hospital, I sat on my pillow in a rocking chair and held Savannah for a few last minutes, bawling and hoping no one would

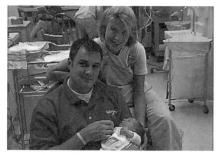

First Family photo, NICU, September 20

notice that visiting hours were over. Finally, Scott said we had to go, so I laid my daughter down in her little metal hospital crib and kissed her goodnight, promising to be back the next morning. Leaving her there was the hardest thing I'd ever had to do. When we got home, I curled up on the daybed in her nursery and cried myself to sleep.

Still, I could not talk to God.

We were awakened the next morning by the telephone. It was the pediatric surgeon calling from the hospital. He wanted us to come and look at the MRI results with him. We skipped showering, drove across town to the hospital, and ran up to the NICU. Dr. Abrams was looking at the scans as we washed our hands and entered the NICU.

"We believe that what you see on the back of your daughter's leg is a tumor. It appears to have originated in the sacrum and grew into the left side of the pelvis and out with the left leg as it

With her "Big Daddy" in the NICU

developed. We think the leg itself was stunted by a cut-off of blood supply and pressure of the tumor. This kind of tumor is called a teratoma, and while it is rare, it is not unheard of in children. We didn't immediately recognize it because we've never seen it occur in utero."

He went on to explain that these tumors are almost always benign—only one-tenth of one percent turn out to be malignant. However, they wanted to have a biopsy as soon as possible to rule out the possibility. We thanked him for his explanation and information, and then sat down to process it.

Our pediatrician came by later to answer any questions we might have. My first one was whether or not we could take Savannah home. It was Thursday morning; she had been in the NICU for almost three days. He was still concerned about the wound on her backside—it was a crater-like adhesion that apparently was the result of the tumor pushing through the skin. He wanted her to stay one more day to make sure it was healing, and he had also noticed a wee bit of jaundice. He hoped to release her the next day.

On Friday, a hospital photographer came by to take Savannah's picture before we went home. *Home?* We didn't know we were going home yet, but he assured us he had received the word, and he snapped a quick shot of her lying on the bed. I still crack up at that picture: I had dressed her in a little blue and white polka-dot gown with a little bird on the chest that looked like Woodstock, and the look on Savannah's face as she squinted and scrunched at the flash of the camera looked remarkably like the little chicken on her chest. It was not her most flattering shot, but we bought it for the outrageous price offered because it marked a huge moment in our lives: we were finally taking her home.

We brought our daughter home on Friday afternoon, four days after she was born. I realize how many parents spend months and months tending to premature and very sick children in the NICU, and I guess we were very lucky, in retrospect. But every second spent in a NICU is torture, and we were euphoric to be leaving. We also didn't know what we were doing. We left the hospital with instructions on how to care for the wound on her backside and an appointment for a biopsy the following Tuesday morning. We bundled her up in a hat, gown, and blanket (even though it was September in South Carolina), tucked her deep inside her plaid car seat, and took a deep breath before pulling out of the parking lot. We had a brand new, tiny, dependent baby who had no idea how clueless her parents were, and she had a tumor that no one here had treated before. *And* we had an appointment for a *biopsy* next week. Scott turned from behind the steering wheel and said, "This just got real."

But ignorance is bliss, and we weren't in the hospital anymore, so we planned to enjoy our baby at home and celebrate our birthdays with our family. We would worry about the biopsy when the time came.

CHAPTER 4

WHEN THE EARTH GIVES WAY

God is our refuge and our strength
An ever present help in times of trouble.
Therefore we will not fear,
Though the earth give way
and the mountains fall into the heart of the sea,
though its waters roar and foam
and the mountains quake with their surging.

~ Psalm 46:1–3

AFTER A GLORIOUS FEW DAYS at home resting and staring at this amazing little creature that now lived in our house, we returned to the hospital early Tuesday morning to check in before the biopsy. We were admitted to a room on the children's ward and told to wait until they called us back to surgery. All four of our parents were there to pray with us before the biopsy. The silent treatment I had been giving God was weighing heavily on me. I was terrified about my baby undergoing surgery at eight days of age. I was scared, and as Scott's dad prayed, I silently lifted up a desperate apology and plea for help.

God, I know I've been hard to get along with lately. I don't even really know what to say to you right now. But please keep my baby safe. Please take care of her in that operating room. I don't deserve anything from you, but please don't hold it against her. Please, God, please help her.

At around 10:30 a.m., a hospital orderly came for Savannah. He walked us through a maze of hallways to the other side of the hospital, and as we came around a last corner, there were two hospital staff in scrubs standing outside a set of swinging doors. They introduced themselves as the anesthetist and the head OR nurse. As they explained what would happen in the operating room, I began to panic. I had the crazy notion to take off running with my baby, but a thread of sanity reminded me that the biopsy would protect her from something worse. And so I held her tight and studied her little face as they finished their spiel. Then the OR nurse turned to me and held her arms out for Savannah. I instinctively pulled her closer as Scott leaned down and kissed her on her forehead. The nurse said, "I promise we'll take good care of her. And we'll call you from the operating room to let you know how things are going. It won't take long." I loosened my grip on Savannah in slow motion and finally released her to the nurse. They turned and walked into the OR with her, leaving us to watch the doors swing behind them. Silently, we turned to walk back to the room. But my legs wouldn't move, and when Scott turned to walk back to me I collapsed into his chest. He leaned back against the wall and wrapped me up in his big arms while we both cried and he prayed.

When we returned to the children's ward, our parents were waiting in the room for us. They made small talk for an hour while we waited for a call from the OR. I don't do small talk well—especially when I'm stressed or worried. So I just sat there silently bargaining with God again until Scott started worrying aloud that it was taking so long. Another hour later, Scott was at the nurses' station trying to get them to call down to the OR for an update. After another twenty minutes, the nurses' station paged us for a phone call. It was Dr. Abrams: the biopsy was a little more involved than they had expected, but she was in the recovery room now and we could go see her.

We ran down the hall, cursed the elevator for moving so slow, and sprinted through hallways to the recovery room. When we got to her bed, I burst into tears. Her little face was swollen, and there were red, raw rectangular patches on her cheeks where tape had been attached to hold tubes in place. She was crying, but her throat was hoarse from the breathing tube they had placed in it during surgery, so her little voice was barely more than a raspy whisper. As soon as I picked her up, she stopped crying and just looked up at me. My heart broke into a thousand pieces. It still makes me cry to think about it. We spent about an hour sitting with her in the recovery area until they released her and let us carry her back to the children's ward.

Again, we sat in the room with our parents and waited for the doctors to give us a report. My daddy had to return to work, but my mom and Scott's parents were all there waiting with us when we heard a knock on the open door and our team of surgeons filled the doorway. Dr. Abrams and his resident stepped inside slowly, still in their OR scrubs. It was 3:00 in the afternoon. In my memory, they both moved in slow motion. Dr. Abrams stepped forward with his head down and shoulders slumped and said, "Mr. and Mrs. Duke, I'm afraid I have some bad news. We've been waiting on the last biopsy report before I came to talk to you, and we just received the last one a few minutes ago. I'm afraid the reports show that the tumor is malignant."

Time stopped. All of us gasped at the same time. I was again sitting in a rocking chair holding Savannah, and I couldn't move. My eyes were locked on Dr. Abrams face, waiting for some really good solution to follow the atomic bomb he had just dropped on us. His usual gruff, booming voice was low and gravelly as he continued. "There are several decisions you'll need to make in the next day or so. The tumor is about the size of a baseball and is roughly a quarter of her body weight. My opinion is that surgery is not an option at this point. I don't think she would survive the operation. The tumor's just too big. I think our best option is to try to shrink it with chemotherapy and hope that she'll grow and become strong enough to withstand surgery in a few months. I've called the pediatric oncologists to come and talk with you this afternoon. I'll be around if you have questions, but I'm sure you need some time right now to digest all of this. Mr. and Mrs. Duke, I'm very sorry."

All of the doctors with him gave us a nod of consolation and looked at the floor as they turned and walked out of the room.

No one said a word. Not a sound. Shock and sorrow filled the room up like a helium balloon, and all of us stared at a different spot on the floor—lost in our own interpretation of what the surgeon had just said. And then slowly, steadily, the words that had been building in me since that first ultrasound finally made their way out of my deepest recesses, up into my throat and out of my mouth. I turned to look at Scott, and I screamed as loud as I could—choking on every word—"*WHERE . . . IS . . . GOD?!*"

Scott all but fell on me, both of us sobbing. Our parents hurried out of our room to leave us alone together. I could hear them crying in the hallway.

I didn't want to talk. We spent the next hour or so writing down questions we needed to ask the doctors. I just kept rocking and looking at the baby in my arms. How could a week-old baby have cancer? *Cancer!* I just kept shaking my head. *No, no, no, this can't be happening. This cannot be happening.*

But soon there was another knock on the door, and the pediatric oncologist introduced himself as Dr. Hayes. He was a jolly, grandfatherly man, and he sat down in a chair beside us and told us how sorry he was to be here with us—that he knew his presence was the last thing a parent wanted. He reviewed with us what the biopsy reports had shown: that the teratoma was very large and would not be able to be removed surgically. Then he began to explain how chemotherapy is administered and the different kinds of treatments that could be used to treat Savannah. He told us there were side effects, but we could talk about that later, after we had had a little more time to recover from all of this. I thanked him. I couldn't take anymore today. He told us he thought we ought to start chemo on the following Monday, and we could call him if we had any questions.

Before he stood to leave, he asked us if we belonged to a church. We told him we were members at First Baptist North Spartanburg. He smiled and said, "Then you'll be just fine. That's a fine church. Wonderful people who will take good care of you. You'll need that.

You'll be just fine." He shook our hands and told us to call the office the next day.

As he left the room, our pastor appeared in the doorway. My mother had called the church office and talked with his secretary as soon as the surgeon gave us the biopsy report. When Pastor Mike got the call from Janice on that awful afternoon, he got up and left a meeting in Columbia and drove an hour and a half to Greenville Hospital, where we sat reeling. He sat down in a rocking chair with us and asked us for an update. We told him, through tears, all that we knew, and he cried with us. And then he said something that has meant more to me and Scott than anything he's ever said from the pulpit. He said he wished he had an answer for us, but that he didn't have any answers. He said he wished he could tell us why this was happening, but he didn't understand why. "But I know one thing," he added, placing his hand on Savannah's head. "I know God loves her more than you love her." Then he closed his eyes and paraphrased the promises of Isaiah 43. "When the waters rise, you will not be swept away. When the fire blazes, you will not be burned." His words were not trite or sent from afar. He was in this with us, and the words came from a deep place of knowing.

Before Pastor Mike left, he told us to call him if we got any other news. He hugged us both, weary and heartbroken at the suffering of his flock.

Later that night, as I lay in the fold-out chair next to the hospital bed where Scott slept, I heard Savannah begin to choke. She was vomiting, and I jumped up and turned her face down, yelling for the nurse to come and help me. She ran in and helped me hold Savannah so that she wouldn't choke because I did not even know how to be a mom yet, much less how to take care of a sick baby in a hospital.

She said the anesthesia from surgery probably just made her stomach a little upset, that nausea is common for twenty-four hours after surgery. As we cleaned her up, I asked her if she knew of kids on the ward who had been through chemotherapy.

She paused. "Actually, my son had lung cancer. He went through months of chemo," she told me as she changed the sheets and I put a clean nightgown on Savannah.

"Oh no, really? How old was he?" I asked.

"He was five," she answered.

"Well, how did he do? I mean, is he doing okay now?"

She hesitated, and I froze.

"Unfortunately," she said, "he didn't make it. He passed away about a year after he was diagnosed."

Hope dropped to the floor like a bowling ball on the tile and bounced several times until it came to rest on the other side of the room.

I lay wide awake all night long, suffocating with fear and panic. I couldn't do this.

The next morning, I asked Scott if he had his Bible. He opened it up, and I asked him to find the passage Pastor Mike had talked about and read it to me. He read it slowly, trying not to be overcome with the emotions we both felt. Since that day, I have

wrapped my arms around this promise and clung to its speaker
with all my might.

> Do not fear, for I have redeemed you;
> I have summoned you by name; you are mine.
> When you pass through the waters, I will be with you.
> And when you pass through the rivers,
> they will not sweep over you.
> When you walk through the fire, you will not be burned;
> the flames will not set you ablaze.
> For I am the LORD your God, the Holy One of Israel,
> your Savior.
>
> ~Isaiah 43:1b–3a

I had nothing left. No strength. No answers. No control. This
wasn't a bad storm we were weathering. This wasn't just flood waters
rising. This was the bottom of the ocean. I didn't even know which
direction to swim to the surface. If I couldn't find God in this, if I
could not find a way to settle this face to face, if I could not trust
Him to carry us to the surface of this deep water, then I was finished.
There was nothing else to hold onto.

And so, over the next few days, weeks, months, I began to search
for Him, to look for Him, to desperately cry out for His help.

And I found Him. Right where He said He'd be.

CHAPTER 5

THROUGH THE FIRE

This third [of the people] I will put into the fire;
I will refine them like silver and test them like gold.
They will call on my name and I will answer them;
I will say, "They are my people,"
And they will say, "The Lord is our God."

~ Zechariah 13:9

BETWEEN OCTOBER 2 AND DECEMBER 7 of 2000, Savannah underwent a series of four cycles of chemotherapy. The plan was something like this: we would check in on Friday mornings, receive the dose of intravenous medicine in the office of the Pediatric Hematology and Oncology Cancer Treatment Center at Greenville Hospital, and then go home and live a relatively normal life until the next cycle three weeks later. The doctors' strategy was to administer three cycles of the treatment and then check the size of the tumor via CT scan to see if it was shrinking. Their hope was that the drugs would either shrink the tumor to a removable size, or that it would keep the tumor the same size as her body grew and became stronger

71

and could withstand the surgery to remove it.

But as with all good medical plans, this one depended on the unique response of the human body, and that can be tricky.

First chemo treatment, 10 days old

Savannah received the first round in the hospital at the end of that first week's stay. We had spent the week there as the doctors tried to determine exactly which drugs might work, requiring numerous scans and tests to measure the exact size and location of the tumor. They also sent slides of the tumor to doctors all across the country for the best opinions. By the end of the week, the treatment was established. They had placed a port into an artery of her heart so that they wouldn't have to continuously try to insert an IV into her tiny baby-veins. I held my breath as the first ounces of chemotherapy eased through the clear tubes and into the chest of my sleeping baby. She was ten days old. I'm not sure what I expected to happen—would it be painful or uncomfortable for her? But she never stirred; she slept through the hour drip until the nurses came to remove the IV. We packed up and went home, where we slept for what seemed like days. Since she had been born, we had spent twelve of her first sixteen days in the hospital.

I had a list of all of the possible side effects from the chemo. Dr. Stroud told me she might experience some nausea the first three or four days, but they couldn't be certain how the medicine would affect individual children. Sometimes they showed no effects at all. He also warned us that the particular drugs they'd be using sometimes caused hearing loss, but we wouldn't know that for a while since she was so young. That was a possibility we couldn't dwell on. We had to keep our focus on getting rid of the tumor and getting through the sickness in the meantime.

After the first week, I thought we were in the clear. She was eating and sleeping well, and everything looked great at her one week checkup.

Then on Monday, ten days after the first dose, she seemed lethargic and uninterested in eating. I called the office first thing that morning and took her straight to the Center, where she immediately had blood drawn. She didn't even cry when they stuck her finger. I knew something was very wrong.

By the time I had walked from the lab to the office upstairs, the nurses had received the lab report and were waiting for me at the door. Savannah's counts were at rock bottom. Her white blood count and hemoglobin counts were dangerously low.

The nurses immediately hooked her up to an IV in the back office for a blood transfusion and boost of antibodies while they scheduled her to be admitted to the hospital. I frantically found a phone to call Scott as the nurse set up Savannah for the IV. After explaining to the school secretary that I did not care what class my husband was in the middle of teaching—I needed to talk to him *now*—Scott answered the phone out of breath and with the sound of fear in his voice. When I heard his voice, I started to cry. It took me several minutes to calm down enough for him to understand me, but he finally said he would be there as fast as he could.

The nurse finished hooking Savannah to the IV and began the blood transfusion as I sat in the rocking chair beside her tiny metal crib. I soon found myself alone in a dimly lit room where I realized numerous kids had received chemotherapy treatments, and countless mothers had sat in this same chair with the same fears suffocating them. I had seen the children in the waiting room, and I wondered if Savannah would lose her hair too.

I picked up Savannah and held her as she slept. I watched an anonymous donor's blood drip, drip, drip into my baby's tiny veins. I wondered if the blood donor ever contemplated who would receive his or her contribution. I thought about whose body it had pulsed through before they showed up for the blood drive.

When the transfusion was complete, we were wheeled through the hospital halls to the Children's Oncology Ward on the third floor. Scott arrived as we were checking in to the room.

We stayed there two more nights for observation. Dr. Stroud explained that, although scary, this was a relatively normal reaction to chemotherapy and they wanted to keep a close watch on her because she was so little. He showed us a tiny vial of a drug called Neupogen that boosts the body's immune system and helps fight off infection when the white blood cells are low. It would help keep her counts from dropping so low after the next cycle. The kicker was that we would have to give her the injections at home.

My knees went weak. As said, I faint at the sight of a needle, and the thought of injecting one into my baby's soft flesh made me woozy. Scott said he would do it, and the nurse came in to show us how and where to administer the injection. The needle was tiny, but the injection had to be given just under the skin of the upper leg or the stomach. My knees melted. I could not stand the thought of sticking a needle into Savannah's tummy. But Scott stepped up and did what needed to be done—a trait he has exhibited time after time in our marriage. He winced as he punctured her skin with the needle; she was so weak that she still didn't cry. But Scott did. I had to walk out of the room.

After another bag of fluids and a day of the antibodies supplement, Savannah perked up, and we were discharged from the hospital. Her next round would start the following Friday.

We started the cycle all over again five days later. And like clockwork, ten days into the treatment she started showing the same side effects. Thank goodness, though, they were much less severe since we started giving her the injections. And, except for the one week out of the three when her counts were low and she needed to stay away from people and potential infections, we had a relatively normal home life. We were warned that if either of us became ill, we would need to be separated from the baby until her immune system was stronger. For the first time since seventh grade, I didn't get bronchitis that year. No one in our house had even a sniffle. Odd, huh?

Basketball season started for both of us in late October, and despite my initial decision to resign for the season in light of the circumstances, Scott and I both decided we could manage to keep our jobs as coaches with the help of our fellow coaches, the players, and our families. Having that outlet for a couple of hours a day kept me from losing my mind. The team, my assistant coach, and I had worked extremely hard the two years prior and had built the program to a level where we were poised for a championship. I relied heavily on my assistant coach, Lillie Young, that year, as well as our athletic director, Deb, and my team. I was distracted and emotional much of the time, and there were bad days when I came to practice straight from the hospital or when Savannah was in the valley of the cycle. My principal and A.D. were gracious to keep me on, considering the amount of time I was absent, but the team provided a support system and distraction I'm not sure I could have survived without.

During one two-week period in mid-November, Savannah vomited every bottle of milk she drank. She couldn't keep anything down for ten days and was hospitalized when she became dehydrated. We and the doctors initially thought that the vomiting was a side effect of the chemo. I can remember lying in bed many nights with Savannah face down on my chest because I was so afraid she would choke on her vomit during the night, and it seemed to be the only position she could sleep in that kept her from throwing up. On those sleepless nights, I would weep quietly and beg God to help us survive this. By this time, she was two months old and had only gained three ounces.

I didn't really know how to take care of a baby that was healthy, much less a baby that was this sick. I was terrified. Thankfully, a resident doctor noticed the symptoms and suggested an ultrasound of her digestive system. It turned out she had a blocked valve in her stomach, a condition called *pyloric stenosis* that kept her food from being digested and produced projectile vomiting. When it was finally diagnosed, she had the surgery to correct it and began eating immediately. It was a fluke condition, occurring in only 3 out of 1,000 infants, and four times more likely in boys than in girls. Like we weren't already battling the odds. Scott says she's stubborn and nonconformist, just like me. Sometimes he makes me cuss.

Up and down, high and low—that's how I remember those first few months. It is amazing to me that I had anything left or that I had any desire to participate in something as seemingly meaningless as a high school basketball season. I sometimes had trouble justifying the amount of time and energy coaching required, and there were numerous days when I told my husband I needed to quit, that I needed to be with Savannah around the clock. But he knows me better than I know myself. He knows I need an outlet when my stress and frustration brew. He knows that my natural tendency is to withdraw under stress, to hole up somewhere and suffer alone, to curl into myself and put up walls. He knew I needed something good in my life that year, something to keep me from collapsing under the sheer weight of our circumstances. I'm not nearly as resilient as he is. He insisted that I finish the season and gladly arranged to keep Savannah during my practices and games. So I relented and threw as much of my energy as I could spare outside the hospital walls into that team. We traded off staying at the hospital while the other led practice. Between treatments, Savannah spent so much time with us in the gym that she could sleep through a crowd of 500 screaming fans without flinching. In fact, the only way we could console her in the hospital sometimes was to turn up the volume on a televised college basketball game. She'd go right to sleep.

There is no question that the twelve girls on my team that season gave me much more than I could offer them. My captains, Nikki and Kenya, were some of our first visitors on the day Savannah was born. The team and parents led the charge to raise money for our medical costs. On the court, they stepped up, were committed to work hard, even on days when I couldn't be there. Leaders emerged on the team who held them all accountable and took much of the weight off of my shoulders. I usually have trouble delegating, but this season I was forced to depend on my supporting staff.

When the third round of chemo was complete in early December, the doctors ordered a CT scan to determine if the chemo had decreased the size of the tumor. I was in my office at the gym getting ready for practice when I got the call from the doctor: the tumor hadn't changed. It was exactly the same size, but Savannah hadn't really grown much either. Because she had been sick for so much of the treatment, she had only gained about six ounces since her birth three months earlier. Dr. Hayes said we'd have to change the treatment. Three rounds of chemotherapy hadn't helped at all.

I couldn't speak. When he hung up, I just sat at my desk with my head in my hands. Our team captain flung open the door looking for the practice uniforms, but I couldn't even look up. Nikki stopped short and walked back outside the office, pulling the door closed behind her.

What would we do now? We had spent nine weeks of chemo and nausea and dehydration, blood transfusions and daily injections—for what?! It had all been a waste of time! When I opened the office door, all of the girls were standing outside waiting to find out what was wrong. Almost in a trance, I told them to go ahead to the gym. I walked upstairs and sat down on the couch in the athletic office. Deb immediately hung up the phone and said, "What is wrong?"

I still couldn't talk. What was there to say? Finally, without emotion, I said, "The tumor's not shrinking. The chemo isn't working." It was the calm before the storm I guess. My emotions were all stirred together into a quiet, bubbling soup that hadn't been taken off the hot eye of the stove.

Deb was asking a thousand questions without expecting an answer, and she called Scott for me and told him to meet me at our house. She told me to go home; she and Lillie would handle practice. On the way to give an explanation to my team, who stood on the baseline waiting for me to start practice, I sat down on the stairs and fell to pieces. When I finally composed myself enough to enter the gym, what they saw was not a disciplined coach but a heartbroken mother who had no masks left to put on. The only thing I remember saying to them is that I needed to be with my family.

That night, my point guard, Nikki, called to check on me.

"We had a really good practice today, Coach. We dedicated today's practice to Savannah."

In mid-December I got a phone call at home from the sports editor at the local paper asking what kind of miracle I had masterminded with the success of the J.L. Mann's girls basketball team. I laughed. *Are you kidding me?* We were 12 and 0, and I had no idea how it had happened except that a diverse band of teenage girls had risen to the challenge of being led by a coach who could barely hold her head up.

I wish those kids knew what a blessing they were to me. They're not kids anymore—they're all adults, some with children of their own by now. But they were a lifeline for me in so many ways. I was amazed and humbled at how those girls rallied around me that season. I still am.

But at the time, in the wake of the disappointing results of the chemo treatments, basketball was the last thing on my mind. My baby still had cancer, and now we had no strategy to rid her of it. The next two and a half months would test my faith in ways I could not fathom. They would bring me to the feet of One who is great enough to move mountains and yet personal enough to sit with us in the valleys.

CHAPTER 6

SHADE TREES

Then the LORD God provided a leafy plant and made it
grow up over Jonah to give shade for his head to ease his
discomfort, and Jonah was very happy about the plant.

~ Jonah 4:6

I LEARNED SO MANY IMPORTANT lessons during the first year
of Savannah's life. But God drew me to himself and changed my perspective most profoundly through the acts of kindness bestowed on
our family by the people of our communities.

As an introvert, there are times when I'd like to live as a hermit
and just hide away from people. *Life would be easy if it weren't for people,*
I think to myself some days. But then I think about how this story
could have turned out without people, and how much my life is en-
riched by said people, and I smack myself in the forehead and go
invite somebody to lunch.

I am convinced that the charge to meet together for fellowship is
not just a good idea but necessary for survival. It's risky in some ways,
but the relationships we build with others ground us in this world. It
gives us a place to belong. It takes work, some vulnerability, a lot of

patience, and tons of grace, but it's worth it. We were made for relationship, after all. So while the idea of being a self-sufficient loner
seems mysterious and intriguing when Jason Bourne does it, having
a strong support network of people who care about you makes life so
much easier and richer. I'm sure Jason Bourne would agree.

We had become enmeshed in a number of pockets within our
community during our first four years of marriage: church, our fellow coaches and teaching staff, the players on our teams, their parents, and the students we taught, the neighbors on our street, as well
as our families and longtime friends. But I resisted building relationships at first. When Scott and I moved into our first house, I made
him hide with me in our living room with the lights off when a
couple from the church we were attending showed up for the obliga-
tory "Wednesday Night Visit." I tried to keep a "professional" relationship between myself and my players and their parents. And when we
moved to Greenville, we kept our garage door closed a lot.

But Scott is an extrovert and needs the social interaction, so he
coaxed me out of my shell and into the world of mingling. We joined
a couples' class at church on Sunday mornings, and I learned how to
flesh out my faith with other believers. I started to open up a little
with my players, let them into my life a little. I became good friends
with some of their parents. I joined the choir at church where I made
lifelong friends at Thursday night worship rehearsals and was men-
tored by watching the lives of men and women who honor God in
all circumstances. We eventually volunteered as Bible teachers in the
college class at First North and poured into the lives of those young
people who had every bit as much impact on our lives as we ever
had on theirs. Our fellow coaches became a second family, the only

friends we had who understood how much time and energy coaching required. We learned that the richest of blessings resides in people—not money or career or fame or possessions—but *people.*

So when the bottom fell out of our world, there were people in place to catch us. We didn't know that's what was happening when we went to dinner with friends, when we sat around in the coaches' office after games or played pranks on fellow teachers or drove to Sonic together after church. We weren't trying to "network" or weave ourselves a safety net. We just did life with people. We let our guards down and loved people and let ourselves be loved. The fact that those were the people who took care of us during tragedy is not a coincidence; it's a natural by-product of sharing your life with others. God wasn't kidding about this. Jesus said we would be known by how we love each other. The people we shared our life with—those tough coaches and reckless teenagers and eccentric neighbors down the street, the alto beside me enduring my joyful noises at rehearsal—we didn't speak about love, we just did it. By showing up for each other and bothering to check on each other and putting in the time to really know each other, love just happened without our knowing it. And love displays itself in a million small ways.

The point of all of this is not that we were a part of every club and society around. I think I've been pretty transparent in saying that all of the "stuff" I was involved in didn't add any integrity or authenticity to my faith. In fact, my busyness in religious activity was a sad substitute for the actual relationship with God I now have. The point of the church is to share life with each other, to help carry each other's burdens. We feel God's embrace through the arms of others. We hear His voice with their concern or kind words. We see Him work through the people who know Him and share His convictions. It seems like something spiritual, even supernatural, happens when people let others into their lives. It requires trust, and much grace, because we all have the capacity to disappoint.

The church has and will continue to burn people when we lose sight of our purpose, which is to love others as Christ loves us. Bad things happen, and we're responsible for that. But far more often than not, the people in my church family are genuine, loving people who are trying, just like me, to grow in character and wisdom and love and to shed the flaws and weaknesses that we all carry around.

I've heard many times that churches are full of hypocrites, and there's no doubt that we fail to practice what we preach sometimes. But, you don't have to be Christian to make that mistake. Like my friend LouLyn says, there are hypocrites at the grocery store and at the bank, but we don't stop going. We're not in this to judge how well someone else actually walks in the direction he or she believes is right and true—it's the effort, the earnestness that matters. For the most part, the people I worship with and grow with are much like friends joining a weight-loss program together: we know how far away we are from the goal, and as we try to shed those extra pounds of sin, bad habits, character flaws, and weaknesses, we cheer each other on toward becoming healthy. And in the meantime, we form strong bonds of unity and friendship that last long past the twenty pounds we lost.

The local church is the tangible body of Christ: the hands, feet, and arms of God. Filling a spot in the back row of a worship service will always feel lonely. It'll always leave a bad taste in your mouth, because you were made for relationship. You'll miss the blessing.

You'll cheat yourself of the supernatural manifestation of God in His people if you don't make it a priority to connect with them.

If there is one thing that I have taken away from this difficult season of our lives, it is this: the power of a seemingly insignificant act of kindness can have tremendous impact on the life of a hurting person. God shows up in the way we take care of each other.

God made Himself known in every single act of love as people came alongside us with selflessness, kindness, and mercy. I will share some of the actions that touched us deeply.

The day after Savannah was born, my sister Heather began to organize meals for us. She contacted all of our friends, teammates, co-workers, and church members, and by the end of the week, she had filled up a calendar for three months solid. This is just how we do it in the South: love is served in a casserole dish and cake plate. We ate meals prepared in the kitchens of people from church, people we didn't even know from other Sunday school classes, parents of kids at school, our neighbors who hardly ever saw us because we spent so much time in the gym or on buses to games out of town, faculty and staff from our schools, fellow altos from the choir, and college kids from church.

On the day of the biopsy, three girls from the college class stood outside our hospital room door while the doctor delivered their devastating news. Those sweet girls left dinner for us in the kitchenette down the hall, understanding it was not a good time to visit. When I was in college, I rarely thought about anyone but myself, so this kind of maturity still stuns me.

When we got the order that Savannah would have to be in quarantine during chemo treatments, these people went out of their way not only to prepare a meal, but to bring it to the hospital *and leave it* without even getting to visit with us. My mind would imagine the hundred other things they had to do that day: taking care of children, working until five, attending meetings, preparing dinner for their own families. The selflessness of these people still makes me weep.

There is significance in Jesus' command to *feed my sheep.* Though we would have been physically able to feed ourselves from the hospital food court, the generous meeting of our physical needs ministered to our spiritual hunger. We were being schooled in the supernatural art of serving others.

For the record, these were not your standard take-to-the-sick-neighbor-casserole dishes. My vivid recollection of the meals we ate is a little bizarre given the stress of the circumstances, but I still remember specific dishes: my neighbor Greta's raspberry vinaigrette salad dressing with feta cheese and walnuts; Deb Grande's beef medallions; Aunt Hilda's eggplant parmesan; Terri Reese's pork tenderloin with green beans. My friend Deidre even went to the trouble of making my mother's recipe for strawberry cake because she knew it was my favorite. These were lavishly generous acts of love, not token efforts. I've never eaten so well in my entire life. And we weren't the only ones eating well. A longtime friend made a conspicuous habit of stopping by our hospital room at dinnertime almost every night, just to check on us . . . and maybe have "just a little" if we had any food left over. The nurses on our hall popped in to see what the dessert of the day would be. We always had much more than enough.

One by one, people took several hours of their day to offer comfort. They came to remind us that we were not alone.

In October, J.L. Mann and Riverside high schools, where we taught, played against each other in a cross-town rival football game. The students of both schools spent the weeks before the game raising money to help us with medical expenses. They held car washes, organized a community yard sale, sold doughnuts between classes, and hosted a slew of other creative fundraisers that only high school students could think up. Teachers from J.L. Mann served dinner and worked the cash registers at Burger King; my basketball players spent a whole Saturday washing cars. At halftime on that Friday night, Scott's friend and fellow coach, Sam, walked us out to the fifty-yard line and presented us with a check for the combined efforts of the student bodies. We carried Savannah high as the crowd cheered her name, and we both cried like babies.

In November, Scott's mom was introduced to a runner named Lansing Brewer. His father had battled cancer for years before his death, leaving his mother in a pit of debt, and Lansing now dedicated his free time to helping families with the financial strain of long-term illnesses. He called my mother-in-law and asked if he could organize and complete a "Love Run" for Savannah. He planned to run across South Carolina, from his hometown of Camden to Greenville where we lived, raising funds along the way. He enlisted help from elementary schools across the state that adopted Savannah and raised money to contribute toward Lansing's Love Run. My scrapbook holds photos of children we have never met gathered in pep rally fashion, holding hand-painted posters that read "GET WELL, SAVANNAH!" Local businesses along the route sponsored the run and collected donations in jars and boxes from the counters of stores in tiny towns like North and Johanna that don't make the map.

On a Friday in mid-November, Lansing laced up his running shoes and embarked on the first of a 133-mile journey toward loving his neighbor. Making brief appearances at the schools and partner businesses along the way, he and his team stopped mid-way at Scott's high school in Columbia where a crowd waited to cheer them on.

By Saturday afternoon, Lansing had completed all but the last leg of the run and arrived with more fanfare than we could have ever manufactured. It was snowing. In South Carolina, where schools shut down at the mere forecast of snow and one or two February flurries a year are celebrated like holidays, a November snowfall is something of a miracle. Lansing entered Greenville County wearing a dusting of snowflakes and was met by the cross country team of J.L. Mann High School, who accompanied him on his last few miles to the school gym. Scott and our family, as well as students from both of our schools and people in the community who had read the story in the paper—all of them welcomed Lansing with applause and cheers of gratitude.

Savannah and I were not present. We were in a hospital room completing her second round of chemotherapy. I sat at the window worrying about the snow and watching the news coverage of Lansing entering Greenville on television while she slept with an IV dripping toxins into the port in her chest. I was conflicted. The attention we were receiving was unnerving, and part of me was relieved that I wasn't in the middle of the hoopla. But I felt guilty about not being there to thank this man. Although there was really no question that one of us needed to be at the hospital with the baby, it seemed improper for me not to be front and center to greet Lansing, to show our genuine appreciation. This was above and far beyond sympathy or mere kindness. He had donated his time and his body, and had united people from all over our state to join him. To help us. I couldn't figure out why he did it. He didn't even know us.

God works in strange ways. While He wrestled me for property rights, He also painted a picture of what love looks like in real life. He spoke in the ears of strangers like Lansing Brewer who listened and made sacrifices to help my family. He whispered our unnamed needs in the ears of people who would move to meet them. He nudged others to visit me, to feed me, to write me, to call me. He set the body of Christ into motion—eyes, ears, hands, feet, shoulders—all pointing in the same direction: the Creator. God was wooing me to Himself through the kindness of His people.

I think most people believe that if they can't help in big ways, small efforts won't really make a difference. This is the biggest lie of all. It's the small things that illuminate most clearly that a divine script is playing out. It was the continuous small acts of kindness that made me think God was trying to tell me something. So if you're thinking your small efforts at encouraging or serving won't matter, let me convince you otherwise.

During Savannah's first three months of life, we spent almost sixty days in the hospital. There are so many details of ordinary, daily life that, in normal circumstances, monopolize our attention. But during those first three months, all those details were insignificant to us. Cutting the grass, dusting the blinds, grooming the dog—those tasks never crossed our minds during long nights in a hospital room. But life continues on with or without our attention, and despite our unawareness of it, there were things that needed to be taken care of. Even the things we knew needed to be done sometimes had to be pushed aside until we were in a position to handle them.

It was these seemingly insignificant details that brought forth everyday heroes in our lives. A high school junior in Scott's psychology class cut our grass when it began to tower over the shrubbery. The father of a kid at school maintained our cars for us. Our neighbors' son made sure our dog, Biscuit, was fed and kept company. The mother of one of my players cleaned my bathrooms once a week. *Cleaned my bathrooms.* Jewels in their crowns, I tell you.

A fifth grader from an elementary school in a neighboring county sent me a card one day explaining how he had used his science fair project to raise money for a little girl with cancer he had heard about. The envelope contained almost sixty dollars and some change and a picture of him in front of his project. I still have the card and his picture in a keepsake box.

The parents of a kid at the school where Scott taught organized a fundraiser at the local Burger King they owned. Hundreds of kids from Riverside, as well as their families, turned up for the event, and it was broadcast on a local radio station during the evening. They donated the proceeds to a fund set up in Savannah's name.

Coincidentally, a semi-professional hockey player named Ryan Stewart had just moved to the area to play for the local Greenville Growl team. On his way around town the next morning, Ryan heard the radio station's recap of the fundraiser the night before, and he decided to help. He and some of the management for the hockey team set up a booth at the stadium where the Growl played their home games, and "Stewy's Corner" began selling hats, t-shirts, and other items to benefit a little girl who had been diagnosed with cancer.

The Booster club at my school donated money for every three-pointer that was scored by the J.L. Mann teams in basketball games that season. It was emotional for me to coach that year anyway, but seeing those signs thrown high over kids' heads in the stands reading "3 for Savannah!" every time we scored a long shot made it hard to concentrate on winning. It felt like we already had.

A lady from the church where I had grown up organized a family barbecue with live entertainment; all of the ticket sales and bake sale proceeds were for Savannah's medical fund.

The track team at J.L. Mann hosted an invitational meet to benefit us, and it included every team in the county. All the runners had t-shirts that announced the Savannah Duke Invitational.

But, out of all of those gestures of kindness, love, and generosity, one stands out. It is almost impossible to believe. On the day before Lansing Brewer's Love Run for Savannah, the newspaper ran a story on the event with a paragraph about our family and Savannah's diagnosis. It was entitled "A Little One's Big Struggle." We were in the hospital that weekend for another round of chemo, and on the afternoon before the run, a couple knocked on our door and asked if we were the family they had read about in the paper. A little embarrassed, I answered *yes*, and they introduced themselves as the parents of a little girl down the hall. Their daughter was also undergoing treatment for a different type of cancer, and they just wanted to let us know that they understood the struggles: their daughter had been diagnosed more than a year earlier. We talked for a long time. They gave us advice about insurance and financial aid, and offered us practical information they had picked up through their experiences. They told us they would be praying for us and would send us some insurance information they thought might be useful.

The next week, we received an envelope from the couple. In it was a sheet of paper with the insurance information they had promised, along with a note that said, "Hope this helps" and a check for the medical fund set up in Savannah's name. I sat on my living room couch and cried and cried and cried thinking about how much of a burden their own medical costs must be, and here they were sending us money to help with ours. My unworthiness was too much to bear.

There is a story in the Old Testament about King David after he defeated the reigning King Saul. In the preceding chapters, Saul had hired David to entertain him but then became jealous of David when God chose him as the next king, spread lies about him, threatened him, hunted him, and repeatedly tried to kill David. David responded with dignity and grace. He never repaid evil with evil. He respected Saul, even at his worst. And when Saul killed himself in the heat of battle, David mourned and wept.

The customary response of a new king was to eradicate any threat of a challenge. Most kings, when they first came to power, immediately had every family member of the preceding royal family killed. But David was different. He was not the leader of a godless nation; he was the anointed king of God's people and a representative of God himself. David does something revolutionary: he shows mercy. Instead of wiping out the seed of the enemy, he demonstrates grace. In 2 Samuel 9,

David is at his table in his palace, in complete power over Israel, when he speaks what surely would have been heresy at the time.

"Is there anyone still left in the house of Saul to whom I can show kindness?"

The ancestor of the Son of man carries out the greatest commandment before it is uttered from the mouth of God: *Do unto others as you would have them do unto you* (Matthew 19:19). Instead of doing what Saul would have done, what other kings would have done, or what all of his men were telling him to do, David chooses to grant kindness, specifically to his enemies. He *looks for* someone he can show kindness, for the sake of his God. He didn't merely pardon or offer a token of generosity—which still would have been above and beyond the call of duty—but he invites Mephibosheth, the only surviving grandchild of Saul, to live in the palace as one of his own sons. The Scripture describes Mephibosheth as "crippled in both feet," his legs damaged as a child when his nurse dropped him as they fled to safety when his father was killed. He had lived years as a disabled fugitive—lonely, damaged, and probably angry and resentful.

But then David sends for him. Imagine the panic that gripped this young man as the king's men knocked on the door. Surely they had come to kill him—had hunted him all these years and had finally come to put an end to his forsaken life. David's men lead him out of the desert, into the royal city, and inside the dining hall where a seat has been saved for him beside the king himself. David rises to greet him—perhaps pulls the chair out for him—and invites him to a feast . . . well, fit for an actual king. The king invites the orphaned, broken Mephibosheth to live with him as royalty. Imagine.

What would our world look like if we all followed David's example? How might our lives, our families, our schools, our churches, our country be transformed if, instead of doing that for which no one could blame us, we did that for which no one had an explanation? How do you explain answering your enemies with kindness? How can you explain helping someone with a financial burden while shouldering your own? Only by following God's example.

Imagine the relief, the humility, the gratefulness Mephibosheth must have felt sitting at the king's table with a plate of roasted lamb and veggies and a glass of the finest wine in front of him. That's what grace feels like.

My family and I have been the humble beneficiaries of an *unreasonable* amount of kindness, generosity, mercy, and grace. All of it was undeserved. What all of these people did for us during those months is hard to fathom, much less to explain. But the crazy truth is that it was becoming familiar—not taken for granted or considered mundane, by any means—but a familiar chorus accompanying each random and seemingly unconnected act of kindness. The students, the teachers, the kids, the runners, the hockey player, the parents—I was beginning to realize that they had all become the voice, the hands, the outstretched arms of God as He sang His songs over me, inviting me to the table, inviting me to reside in His royal presence:

"Do not fear, Zion;
do not let your hands hang limp.
The Lord your God is with you,
the Mighty Warrior who saves.
He will take great delight in you,

in his love he will no longer rebuke you,
but will rejoice over you with singing."

~ Zephaniah 3:16b–17

From time to time, I think about those kids at the elementary schools along the route of Lansing's Love Run. They've all finished high school by now. I wonder if they've ever thought again about the money they turned in to their homeroom teacher, or the little girl they made posters for. I think about it. I think about the kid and his science fair project, the hockey player, the students and teachers, the neighbors --all the people, with and without names I know, who God lined up like lights on a runway, all pointing to Him.

Here I Am. Here I Am. Come this way. Land here. This is the way.

Every time I think about all of the wonderful people who helped us during that time, I end up thinking of Jonah. Weird, I know. But I read the end of the story of Jonah a few years back, and I was over-taken by God's unrelenting, unwavering love for His children and how He orchestrates people and circumstances to bring them back to Himself.

As recorded in the Bible, Jonah was a prophet God had chosen to voice His thoughts to His people, and he lived in a safe, quiet town called Jerusalem. Then God suddenly tells him to go to the country of Nineveh with a message. To a nation known for violence, wicked-ness, and cruelty, God sent Jonah to say *Repent from your wickedness or be destroyed*. That is a tough assignment. Jonah had not applied for this job. He was quite content being the top prophet in town, in a city and nation protected and blessed by the standards set by God, and he had no intentions of delivering a message like that to a bunch of godless thugs, murderers, and warmongers. It was ridiculous. It was risky. There was nothing in it for him. And what would his religious friends and fellow prophets think about him associating with dirty Ninevites? His holy reputation would be ruined. Those people were hopeless. Truly. So Jonah did what any sensible person would do—he caught a ship sailing in the opposite direction and tried to sleep it off. Been there, done that. Really, God wouldn't call someone to do something *dangerous* or *illogical*, would He?

The rest of the story has been included in every Sunday school class curriculum since forever. Jonah was swallowed by a whale at sea, and after three days, the fish spit him onto the beach where he picked seaweed and fish bones out of his hair and remembered who he worked for. There's nothing like a good dose of humility to remind us Who's in charge.

Jonah begrudgingly headed toward Nineveh to deliver the suicide bomb. His best hope was a quick and painless death. But something miraculous happened. When he spoke God's message and braced himself for the reaction, the hopeless foreigners wept and mourned as they recognized truth and realized the name of the darkness that smothered their hearts: *Sin.* They *believed* the message Jonah delivered. They turned from their wicked ways toward the God they'd never heard of. No one had ever told them He existed. Jonah walked away unscathed and became one of the first missionaries of the gospel, of the most important message ever sent: there is a God who loves us and desires us to be free from the sin that wrecks our lives. He invited the worst of the worst to the table.

But Jonah is not happy about it. As the Ninevites celebrated their newfound salvation and new way of life, Jonah walked away, unharmed but bitter that those wicked people had escaped punishment. They didn't get what they deserved. After all of those years of killing and fighting and stealing, they get a clean slate?! This wasn't right. It wasn't justice.

So Jonah headed for a hill overlooking the city, hoping that maybe God was just pausing for effect. He waits, and waits, and waits, and . . . nothing. As he sits in the heat, his blood beginning to boil in anger, God causes a tree to grow over Jonah to give him shade from the sun.

Can you believe that? That part just gets me. Not only did Jonah run from God and deliberately disobey him, but now he's sitting like a big spoiled punk, pouting that those poor people didn't get demolished! What a pious, rotten jerk! And what's worse, he doesn't even notice the tree that God planted to shade him.

And then I realized—I was Jonah.

I could hear myself saying, *This isn't fair . . . why is this happening?* I too had been giving God the silent treatment as I sat in the shade of all these trees He had planted in my life. All these kind, generous people—did I really think they all just showed up accidentally? Did I really believe that just because I had given up on God, He would stoop to my level by giving up on me? When God promises in Jeremiah 29:11 that "He has loved me with an everlasting love," He means it. He's not leaving me—no matter what I do or don't do, regardless of my good days and bad days or the big fat spoiled baby attitudes—He's not leaving me. I can't shake Him, no matter what I do.

Don't get me wrong; sometimes His presence is a firm pressure to guide me in the right direction. Sometimes it's a swift kick to the backside. And then sometimes it's the soothing melody of a lullaby during a sleepless night. But He's not leaving me. I've been convinced.

Sitting under the shade trees He had planted in my life, I learned much about the character of God. He's stubborn. More stubborn than Jonah, and more stubborn than me. He's relentless in His pursuit of us—in proving Himself over and over and over. It's hard to wrap my mind around this in the culture we live in where remaining cool and detached is the fashion and abandoned love is a faux pas. But God just puts His heart right out there for the taking.

I was learning of His unrelenting, unashamed, unreasonable love for me in spite of my unfaithfulness to Him. I had cut Him off, turned my back, and stuffed my fingers in my ears. Yet still, He kept coming after me. Still, He kept sending me love notes and shade trees.

I don't know what happened to Jonah. The story never tells us. I imagine he went on to a pious but joyless life instructing people on the things of God without ever understanding his heart. But I know how I want my ending to be. I want to live like David—looking for someone to whom I can show God's kindness. My life has been forever changed by people who did this for us. They stood up over us to shield us with kindness, casting on us the shadow of the Most High. Those shade trees are a reminder of a God who is *enormous,* the God who sees us and will never leave us. The sight of my daughter's face helps me remember to be grateful for the kindness of others, to return the favor shown to us. I want my life to be a shade tree—a shelter from the heat of life, planted by God, at just the right time.

CHAPTER 7

THE FIRST WAVE

"I have told you these things, so that in me you may have
peace. In this world you will have trouble. But take heart! I
have overcome the world."

~ Jesus in John 16:33

IT WAS THE SECOND WEEK of December. For lack of a better plan,
the oncologists decided to start a second cycle of three sets of chemotherapy treatments, mainly to try to keep the tumor from growing
until we had a better strategy. We had spent the previous weekend
in the hospital receiving her fourth round of chemo. But after the
oncologists and surgeons discussed Savannah's situation, they con-
cluded that surgery was inevitable and that our local hospital was not
equipped to handle the kind of operation she would need. All agreed
that Duke University was the best choice, and the sooner the better,
so we were scheduled to meet with doctors there on December 15.

So on Wednesday night of that same week, we made the four-
hour drive to Durham, North Carolina to meet with a slew of doctors
from the Duke Medical Center. All day Thursday and Friday were
spent making stops with different doctors all over the campus: a

pediatric orthopedist, a pediatric urologist, a pediatric general surgeon, two different pediatric oncologists, and a plastic surgeon. In the midst of all that running around, we were completely clueless about how all of this was going to come together—we just knew it was the only hope we had of helping our baby. In retrospect, I am amazed at how a team of different doctors and specialists somehow synchronize their schedules and work together to save the lives of strangers.

Dr. Henry Rice was the pediatric surgeon, and he would essentially head up the team of doctors working together on this operation. We were immediately put at ease when we met him. His gentle handling of Savannah and his friendly demeanor gained our trust. The Duke medical team decided they would surgically remove Savannah's tumor in February. Dr. Rice agreed that her chances were better if she gained some weight, and the oncologists agreed that chemotherapy treatments should be stopped at once. Dr. Rice explained how the surgery would take place, and which parts of the operation each doctor would participate in. And then he told us some of the risks involved.

With gentleness and sensitivity, he explained that the tumor was in the pelvis and was virtually touching every internal organ below her waist. It was about the size of a baseball, and taking it out would mean maneuvering around all of her reproductive and digestive organs. He wanted to make sure he informed us that he could not guarantee that the internal organs would not be damaged during the surgery but that he was very confident it could be done. That was the first time we had considered the risks involved. I finally asked the question we had been tip-toeing around since we arrived: *Was there a chance she could die in surgery?*

I couldn't have been the first parent to ask him that question, and he answered it like the professional that he is: there is always a chance of losing a patient in any surgical operation, but this was a strong team of doctors, and he had chosen to work here largely because of the excellence of the hospital and its support staff. He was confident that the surgery would be successful.

That was the best we could ask for.

Dr. Rice was our first appointment during those two days, and so the rest of the trip was spent following directions to all the other offices. On Friday, though, we had a two-hour break between appointments, so Scott suggested we go over to Duke University's basketball facilities.

This had been his ultimate goal all along. We had been Duke basketball fans for years—long before we were referred to Duke Medical University. I actually think I noticed Scott's eyes light up when our doctors recommended that we come here. He wasn't excited about the circumstances that warranted our trip to Duke, but if we've *gotta* travel to another hospital, it might as well be somewhere we might possibly run into the legendary Coach Mike Kryzewski.

We drove over to the home of the Blue Devils that afternoon and stood in the back parking lot of Cameron Indoor Stadium to take a few lame pictures outside the castle-like building. A car pulled up nearby, and in a scene that should have been in slow motion with background music, the All-American forward, Shane Battier, got out of his car, pulled out his gym bag, and said hello to us on his way into practice. Scott had this bizarre expression on his face that made me think he might run down Battier and tackle-hug him.

"Do *not* ask him for an autograph," I hissed without moving my mouth.

"I'm not going to ask him for an autograph," Scott said, flashing his sideways smile that makes me nervous. I thought we were heading back to the car when he stopped and said, "Let's just go see if the doors are locked." He turned and started toward the entrance.

"*No!*"

But my husband's mantra is "Better to ask forgiveness than for permission," and I knew this was going to be an utterly mortifying experience. On the other hand, Scott has never been embarrassed that I know of, nor has he ever found a door he couldn't open or a place he couldn't talk his way into, so I knew there was no stopping him now. Lo and behold, the doors were unlocked, and he motioned for me to follow him as he stepped inside.

"No—don't do it!" I whispered *really loud* and motioned him vehemently back toward the car, but he grinned and disappeared beyond the giant wooden doors. So there I was. I could either stand by myself in the parking lot holding my three-month-old baby in the cold, or I could follow my husband's lead into who-knows-what kind of humiliation. Decisions, decisions. I rolled my eyes and stomped after him.

I slowly cracked the enormous doors enough to peek inside the lobby. There was no one around but my dear husband sneaking around in the hallway. He heard the door close behind me and said, "Hey, let's go down to the gym and take some pictures."

"Are you crazy?" I said. "There's a word for that here. It's called *trespassing.* Would you mind if we tried to avoid going to jail with our newborn?"

"Oh, come on. Nobody's gonna care if we're here. Let's just look around."

There was no talking him out of it. We wandered down the stairs and onto the hardwood floor where our beloved Blue Devils battle their opponents. I've never actually been to a Duke game, but it was cool to stand on the free throw line imagining the Cameron Crazies cheering us on. I kept my eyes peeled for security guards, but only a polite team manager finally approached us to let us know the team was about to start practice. We actually took some great pictures on the gym floor before they ran us out. I do have to confess that it was pretty cool to see all those great basketball players up close. We acted like they were our personal best friends when they won the national championship at the end of that season.

We burst out of the outer doors laughing and a little exhilarated by our breaking-and-entering adventure. Then I punched Scott in the arm and told him never to do that to me again.

We finished our round of doctor consultations and finally arranged the details of the surgery before we drove home late that afternoon. We made plans to return for surgery on February 5. In the meantime, we needed to "get some meat on that baby's bones." It was the best assignment we'd ever been given.

We spent Christmas break without any more hospital stays. Scott and Savannah traveled with our girls' basketball team to a tournament in Savannah, GA, where we also visited Scott's family. The respite from hospital stays was an enormous relief, a glimpse of normal. It was the first time we had spent any time together without worrying about blood counts or Neupogen injections or chemo drips.

We celebrated Savannah's first Christmas at home with no drama, no crises, and lots of joy and rest.

But by the end of December, Savannah was still so tiny. Pictures from those first three months break my heart. Her skin looked so thin and pale, and she had lost almost all of her hair by then. I'm not even sure I realized how sick she looked until later.

But in January? Well, in January, Savannah made up for lost time. I guess her body just began to thrive when the chemotherapy was out of her system, because she swelled up into the chubbiest, happiest baby you've ever seen. Pictures from those next two months make me literally laugh out loud. Scott had been sending out photos of Savannah and prayer requests and updates over the last few months, and there were people who had let us know early on via email that they had Savannah's picture on their refrigerator or on their desk at work, praying for her constantly. So when we sent out the new pictures of what we refer to as her "chipmunk stage," we actually got responses that they too had laughed out loud at the pudgy, bouncing baby girl on the screen.

What a transformation! Not only did she swell physically, her personality began to blossom as well. She had always been a sweet-tempered baby, but she was suddenly this happy, joyful, outgoing baby girl who laughed and brought smiles to all who laid eyes on that dimple in her left cheek. Her eyes sparkled. She cackled when she laughed and squealed in delight. We were smitten.

I began to offer up quiet words of thanks. Grateful for the chance to finally see my baby thrive, my heart's walls melted a little every time I heard Savannah laugh. I knew God had to be in this. He knew that Scott and I needed that time with Savannah before February arrived. He knew we would need something to fight for.

The conference basketball season rolled on, and our girls' team was surpassing all expectations. By the time we left for Duke on February 4, we were only a couple of games away from clinching the regular season title. But I had to leave that responsibility to the girls and my assistant coach. All of my mental and physical energy would be required for the real-life battle we would face the next day.

Scott and I arrived at the Brookwood Inn across the street from the hospital on Sunday, February 4, to check in and unpack before we registered at the hospital. Scott's dad, "Big Daddy," was waiting there when we arrived. He had brought a gift for his granddaughter: a small gold medallion of a guardian angel to hang from her hospital crib. It hangs from her bedroom doorknob today.

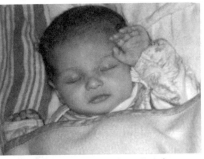

Last chemo treatment. At almost 3 months old, she had gained only a few ounces.

We checked in at the hospital, and as soon as we were settled in the room, a nurse came in to start a "cleansing procedure."

6 weeks after stopping chemo

It was a small plastic tube that was inserted into Savannah's nose and down her throat to drip medicine into her stomach so that her digestive system would be cleaned out before surgery in the morning. It was miserable. She cried all night, and I cried every time I looked at the horrible tube coming out of her nose. None of us slept much.

In the morning, all of our family had arrived and crowded into the tiny room to pray over her. I was still having trouble voicing my feelings to God, but I listened closely as our parents prayed aloud, and I silently prayed for God to honor their prayers, and if He could hear my heart, to please help us.

It was like a parade to the OR. Scott carried Savannah, with me holding on to his arm, and the rest of our family following behind. They all kissed her before we took her back, and she flashed them a big, sleepy smile as we walked through the swinging doors. My father-in-law is a big, tough guy, but I think that nearly toppled him.

We were led back to a tiny waiting area behind a curtain, and a nurse brought in some consent forms for us to sign while we waited for the surgeons to make preparations. When she left, I picked up the clipboard and looked over the form. On it, Dr. Rice had handwritten the potential risks we were asked to acknowledge before they would perform the operation. I had heard this all before, but somehow, seeing it there in black and white made potential risks seem like enormous dangers. I read them slowly: *tumor resection, possible hysterectomy, possible removal of bladder and/or parts of the rectum, colon or intestines . . .*

Hysterectomy? It had never occurred to me that she might not be able to have children after this surgery, even though Dr. Rice clearly explained that some of the internal organs and reproductive system might be damaged. I just hadn't put it all together.

I couldn't read anymore. I handed the clipboard to Scott and asked to hold Savannah for the next few minutes. He winced as he read, and looked up at me with a hurt expression.

Soon the nurse came for us, and we walked back to the OR doors. Once again, someone in scrubs reached for Savannah, and again, I instinctively drew back. Scott kissed the baby and whispered something in her ear, then told me to give her a kiss before he took her from my arms, squeezed her tight, and handed her to the OR nurse. We walked to a small family waiting room and fell apart. It was 6:30 a.m.

There was a larger waiting room in the surgical lobby where our family waited for us. They had brought board games to occupy the time, since Dr. Rice estimated the surgery would last twelve hours. But I didn't want to play games. I was useless in Trivial Pursuit, which is my favorite game. My father-in-law still likes to chalk that one up as an epic defeat over me, and I like to make him feel guilty about beating a grieving mother while she's down. We tend to have a highly competitive relationship, but I gladly surrendered that day. I couldn't have cared less.

From time to time, the phone would ring, and they would call our name. "Duke family?" One of us would get an update from the OR. My cousin Ginger, who had made the trip with my sisters, walked with me around the floor, talking and trying to keep my mind occupied.

By three o'clock, we were exhausted. Then another phone call was announced, and the receptionist said the doctor would be out to see us shortly. *Which doctor? Was something wrong?* My heart was pounding in my throat when Dr. Rice poked his head out of a small conference room and motioned us inside. All eyes were on us as Scott reached for my hand and led me through the door. We sat down in front of Dr. Rice and didn't say a word as he explained exactly what they had been doing in the OR. She had required a couple of blood transfusions, but she had done well . . . there appeared to be no damage incurred to the internal organs or reproductive system . . . they had been able to salvage the healthy part of the leg so that there might be a potential for a prosthesis . . . she was in recovery now.

We just sat there. His eyebrows were raised high over his dark eyes, and he was smiling expectantly, but we didn't move or make a sound.

"Mr. and Mrs. Duke?"

We nodded.

"We got it. We got the tumor. This is really good news. The operation was completed without a hitch." He still looked back and forth between the two of us with his eyebrows raised.

"Okay, so," Scott paused, "you're saying that everything is good?"

"Yes. This is the best case scenario. I know you've had a lot of bad news since your daughter was born, but, Mr. and Mrs. Duke, the surgery was a success. We got the tumor." He patted us both on the shoulder on his way out and, before he closed the door, added with a smile that we could go up to the recovery room soon to see her.

And then I started to cry.

Still in a stupor, we let our families know about the surgery, and we all walked around the hospital and up to the pediatric ICU where she would be taken. When I saw her sweet face—swollen and puffy from the surgery and marked again with tape and tubes—I almost could not bear it. I didn't even have the urge to cry, just a wave of grief and sorrow at seeing my baby that way. We had to leave her in the care of the nurses that night, since there was no place for us to stay in the ICU. Our families gave her kisses before we left.

I said another prayer of thanks late that night, lying in bed, and marveled at how God had shown up once again. *Why would He continue to show Himself to me when I constantly doubted and turned from Him? How did He always know exactly what I needed and when? Why did He bother to go to so much trouble to make sure I noticed His handiwork, when it was obvious I wasn't paying attention?* I couldn't explain His perseverance—this holding on to me when I clearly had tried to yank away. I got up, turned on the light, and reached for Scott's Bible on the nightstand. He turned over and covered his head with a pillow as I flipped through the Psalms and found the words of my recovering heart:

> You have searched me, LORD, and you know me.
> You know when I sit and when I rise;
> You perceive my thoughts from afar.
> You discern my going out and my lying down;
> You are familiar with all my ways.
> Before a word is on my tongue you, LORD, know it completely.
> You hem me in behind and before;
> and you lay your hand upon me.
> Such knowledge is too wonderful for me, too lofty for me to attain.
> Where can I go from your Spirit?

Where can I flee from your presence?

If I go up to the heavens, you are there.

if I make my bed in the depths, you are there.

if I rise on the wings of the dawn; if I settle on the far side of the sea,

Even there your hand will guide me; your right hand will hold me fast.

~ Psalm 139:1–10

CHAPTER 8

SUNSHINE ON OUR FACES

But you, LORD, are a shield around me, my glory, the One who lifts my head high.

~ Psalm 3:3

WE LEFT DUKE UNIVERSITY MEDICAL Center a week after that first major surgery. A friend of a friend sent a private plane for us so that Savannah wouldn't have to make the trip home strapped in a car seat, sitting on her stitched-up backside. Because of the area where the tumor had been resected, the doctor had temporarily rerouted her bowels with a colostomy until the wound healed completely. We spent a great deal of time with nurses teaching us how to change the bag and the dressings for the healing wounds. Our ordinary diaper bag was replaced by a backpack organized with all the medical supplies necessary for Savannah's significantly more complicated daily care.

Even though those next six weeks were full of doctor's appointments and wound dressings, Savannah was growing and thriving and loving life. She was a different child than the one we handed over to the surgeon six weeks earlier. Her green eyes twinkled in the sunshine, and the dark hair she had been born with had given way to golden blonde strands that were not quite long enough to finish off with a bow, despite my persistent efforts. My basketball team rolled along to clinch the regular season championship, and Savannah became our team mascot. Through the playoffs, she sat on her daddy's lap in the stands and learned to clap to the rhythm of "DE-FENSE, DE-FENSE" chanted by the crowd. By the time our almost perfect season ended at the Upper-State championship game in a loss to Seneca, our five-month-old had been to more ball games than most people attend in a lifetime.

By the end of March, Savannah was six months old, and it was (finally) time to return to Duke to have the colostomy removed. Hal-le-lu-jah! We celebrated that milestone almost as much as the tumor resection. Although the colostomy reversal was a surgical procedure and she was again put to sleep, it felt like a routine doctor's visit compared to the traumatic experiences peppering the first six months of her life. She was in the recovery room entertaining the nurses within an hour after we handed her over to the surgical team, and we only had to stay in the hospital a day and a half until the doctor was sure her bowels were functioning properly. I never imagined such joy over a dirty diaper.

It was the first weekend of April when we checked out of Duke Medical Center. We left the hospital and drove straight to Myrtle Beach, where we stayed at a friend's family condo and had the time of our lives. I can't express what joy and relief we felt that week in the sunshine and salt air with our baby for the first time. It felt like we were finally out from underneath this cloud Savannah had been born under.

Spring and summer were blissful. Savannah cut her first tooth at Tybee Island while we were on vacation with my parents and sisters; we swam like fish in my parents' pool all summer long and spent hours at the park or zoo on play dates with friends. In July, when she was ten months old, she pulled herself up to stand for the first time, well after all the other mothers I knew boasted their child's first steps. I took pictures and recorded the scene in my scrapbook:

"Taking a Stand" July 26, 2001, 10 months old

Pulling up to stand was not an easy feat for you. You don't have two legs to balance like the rest of us; you need twice the strength and effort to do the things we take for granted. But you are persistent, even now—a trait you will need every day for the rest of your life.

I came into your nursery on this day, a Thursday, and found you standing for the first time in your crib. You would have thought I found you climbing Mount Everest! With you, my baby, the little things are miracles, and there are very few things in your life that I take for granted. I pray that God will show me a new miracle in you every day that he entrusts me with your life.

I love you, Baby Girl.

There was much growth and sunshine that summer. I began attending a Bible study one night a week and committed myself to really getting to know God through His Word. I knew with certainty that He had been at work in my life. I had seen His hand on the moments and events of the last year, and I felt the need to immerse myself in Him. To snuggle up close and get to know Him again, maybe for the first time. My soul had been so parched and ragged for the last few years, and I was thirsty for the life I was finding in His Word. I drank it in.

The sunshine personified the joy and relief we all felt. We enjoyed every second of that summer. But it did not last long enough.

CHAPTER 9

THE BACK SIDE OF THE STORM

Shall we accept good from God and not trouble?

~ Job 2:10b

IN EARLY SEPTEMBER, DR. RICE'S office called from Duke to set up a follow-up appointment. And on September 17, the day before Savannah's first birthday, we made the four-hour drive back to Durham for her checkup.

I watched the bleeding trees as we sped past them along the interstate. The leaves had already begun to change colors along northern I-85. The summer sun had stained the leaves gold, auburn, and crimson, and the branches would soon let go. Autumn is a welcome relief to the "dog days" of South Carolina summers, although it never comes soon enough. But there's something sad about the season. It's as if the summer just doesn't have anything left to give and so surrenders itself to winter lurking in the distance. Autumn feels like the world is giving up.

The next morning we reported to the radiology department where the scheduled MRI was conducted on Savannah. Scott and I read magazines in the waiting room for the hour-and-a-half procedure, and were called back to pick her up only to find her entertaining the nurses in the recovery room. We had an early lunch afterwards, and then made our way to Dr. Rice's office that afternoon. When the nursing staff realized it was Savannah's birthday, they lavished her with more toys and gifts than we could pack in our car. The lab draws earned her a toy doctor's kit and a stuffed Ernie from Sesame Street (covered with Band-aids and bandages) as the nurses tried to earn Savannah's forgiveness for sticking her.

We finished up in Dr. Rice's office for our final appointment. We all shook hands and he commented on how much Savannah had grown and changed. Then he took us around the corner where he clipped Savannah's MRI film to a light box. He showed us three different films: one showed the tumor before he removed it in February. Its presence seemed vulgar and grotesque, filling the pelvic cavity with its cancerous body. I was glad those times were over. The second film he held to the light showed her pelvis and lower abdomen after the surgery had removed the tumor in February. We could clearly see the pelvis and hipbone and some of the vital organs that had been compressed by the tumor before it was removed.

"Yayyy!" I sang quietly to Savannah, lifting and bouncing her up and down as if she'd just won the Super Bowl.

As he took the second film down, he turned to us and began to talk about the statistics of recurrence and some other information that caused my face to scrunch up in confusion. *What was he saying?* He continued to talk as he pinned the last film to the light behind it, and we saw again a giant white blob filling the lower half of her inner body. *You just showed us this,* I thought to myself.

I interrupted the stream of words coming out of Dr. Rice's mouth because they were disintegrating before they reached my brain, and said, "I'm sorry, Dr. Rice—what is this we're looking at?"

He paused and said, "These are the images from today's MRI." He pointed to the date in the top corner: *09-18-2001*. "It appears," he continued, "that some residue of the tumor was not completely removed during the resection, and the tumor has regenerated. It's larger than the last tumor. It's growing, fast. We now have to decide how and where to take this one out, but we need to do it as soon as possible." Or something like that.

I have no memory of what happened after that. I don't know if we went back to his office, or what we talked about, or anything else except that the tumor had grown back and we were going to have to do this thing all over again. So I'll have to use my husband's memory here. Apparently, Dr. Rice made some phone calls, because at some point over the next few hours (or maybe days—I don't know), he suggested that we see a surgeon named Dr. Richard Azizkhan at Cincinnati Children's Medical Center. Dr. Rice had trained under Dr. Azizkhan, and he believed this doctor was the best choice for the kind of surgery it would take to make sure there was no residue of the tumor left behind.

Obviously, we checked out and drove home. I'm sure we talked about this new bomb that had been dropped on us, but I don't remember any of that. I just kept thinking, *It's her birthday. It's her first birthday.*

In the biblical account of Job, the man has just received word that he has, over the course of an afternoon, lost his livelihood, his wealth, and all of his children in three consecutive and unforeseen disasters. His response is startling. Unnatural. Even unsettling for me at times. Upon hearing that his adult children have all been crushed to death at the oldest brother's house during a celebration, Job tears his clothes, shaves his head, and then *falls to the ground in worship.*

"He fell to the ground in worship and said, The Lord gave and the Lord has taken away. May the name of the Lord be praised" (Job 1:20–21).

This stuns me. Like skeptics of faith, I admit that there is an immediate reaction in me that says, *That's just not a natural, human response to a tragedy like this.* Real people don't say things like that. It doesn't match up with the five stages of grief or anything else that we've been taught in our psychologically saturated and emotionally intelligent culture. Cry, scream, fling yourself onto your bed, and cry yourself to sleep. We want to hit something. Or someone. And when we just can't cope with all those overwhelming emotions, we turn to Valium or wine or painkillers and sleep away the first half of the grief process.

I've had all those emotions, and most of those responses. And yet, as I looked out the window on that drive home from Durham, red, gold, and orange leaves blurring together along the highway, this passage of the Bible flickered in my mind. I didn't know the specific passage, but I knew the principle: Job praised God not only for the good things, but for the bad too. *How do I get to that point?*

I had been asked, several weeks earlier, to give my testimony at a choir concert at our church. Our minister of music asked me if I would tell what the Lord had done in our family's life since Savannah had been born. I joyfully agreed, eager for the opportunity to praise God publicly for His goodness and mercy toward us. I wrote and rewrote what I wanted to say, because I had a five-minute time limit and *how could I whittle the last year into five minutes?* I had almost memorized the testimony already. I would be standing in front of 2,000 people in our sanctuary, so I didn't want to wait until the last minute to try to think of something to say.

The concert was the following Saturday. What was I supposed to say now? How could I give a testimony after receiving devastating news—*again?* And then Job echoed, "Shall we accept good from God and not trouble?" (Job 2:10).

I had to make a choice. During that road trip home, I decided that I had to praise God for what He had already done for us, and to trust Him to take care of what was ahead of us. I would thank Him for the good. I could not deny the mercy and the protection and the provision He had given to us simply because there was trouble ahead. How could I *change* my testimony? I was a witness to what God had done in our lives. I didn't have any doubts about what I knew had happened. Did my circumstances now change those facts or alter the character I had seen of God? I could not deny what had already happened, regardless of what might happen in the near future.

I gave that testimony in front of a full sanctuary on Saturday night, September 23, five days after hearing that my daughter's cancer had returned. It was a turning point in my life.

Over the next couple of weeks, we talked via telephone to a whole host of doctors whose opinions we needed to decide the next move. Dr. Rice was willing to perform the surgery at Duke, but he believed that Cincinnati Children's had a more comprehensive team of doctors who would be needed for this kind of surgery. Basically, he said, there were two options, and the best wouldn't be determined until the surgery was in process. First, once he was inside the area and had removed the bulk of the tumor, he would be able to decide whether or not the hip and partial femur could be saved. Ultimately, if the tumor was in the joints of the bones of her lower side, the hip and femur would need to be removed completely to ensure complete resection of all the "margins" of the tumor. If, however, he could see no evidence of any tumor in the joint or bones, he might be able to save the bony structure on that side.

My fear was that if all the bony structure was removed, she would never be able to have a prosthesis as she grew old enough to walk. Dr. Rice said that was indeed a concern and that they would do everything possible to remove the tumor and save the hip and femur for that very purpose, but ultimately Savannah's life depended on getting rid of every trace of the tumor.

Dr. Rice's real concern was that the support staff at Duke would not be able to accommodate such an extensive surgery, despite its stellar reputation and top-notch facilities. The last surgery had lasted nine hours and necessitated multiple blood transfusions, and he was just unsure whether the relatively small medical center could handle a more complicated surgery than the first one had been. Dr. Rice had worked under an experienced surgeon at Cincinnati Children's Hospital and trusted him as one of the best pediatric surgeons in the country. He strongly encouraged us to visit Cincinnati and Dr. Azizkhan in order to make the most informed decision possible.

I didn't want to meet a new team of surgeons or be that far away from home. But we weren't exactly in a position to argue, and we trusted Dr. Rice's judgment. His office called Dr. Azizkhan's team to set up an appointment, and the following Sunday we flew to Cincinnati.

Luckily, my husband has a great friend who had just moved to the Cincinnati area and was happy for us to stay with him during our visit. Shane picked us up from the airport, and on Monday, we had an itinerary packed with six different appointments in six different parts of the sprawling hospital complex, all scheduled within an hour and a half of each other. Like every other doctor's visit we've ever had, every office was running behind, and we were later and later to each appointment. In that one day, Savannah had a CT scan, a VCUG (which is a torturous bladder test), an ultrasound of her bladder and kidneys, and appointments with an orthopedic surgeon and urologist. We had no time to stop and eat lunch as we sprinted through the halls and checked in late to every appointment. Savannah screamed her head off every time the orthopedic surgeon looked at her, and the ultrasound and VCUG were invasive and painful for her. She screamed through every appointment until the next-to-last office visit with the urologist, where she finally fell asleep from exhaustion. By the time we arrived to the waiting room of the head surgeon, Dr. Azizkhan, we were two hours behind schedule, starving, and thinking this was a series of bad signs. In the moment, we'd have rather been anywhere but Cincinnati. We were tired and irritated and at our wits' end. I was thinking that if this doctor or receptionist told me we were too late to be seen, I would most definitely lose my religion in this waiting room. Security would probably be called because I was not leaving until we saw this doctor! I prayed, *Lord, please let this go smoothly. I can't take much more today. Please help us get in and out of here quickly so we can go home, and please give us some sign if this is where we're supposed to have this surgery.*

Finally, a smiling nurse appeared in the doorway and called Savannah's name, holding the door open for us and then leading us to a small office down the hall. It was almost 6 p.m. Savannah had just awakened in the waiting room and was still tired and cranky from not getting a full nap, and I prepared myself for more drama and trauma should this next doctor poke and prod her some more. But then the door opened, and a very distinguished looking, grandfatherly man came in and shook our hands and greeted us in a low, gentle voice that immediately put us at ease. I swear the air around him glowed, and angels sang in the background. As he bent down to say hello to Savannah, she immediately held her arms out for him to pick her up. He held her for the rest of the appointment. I felt like I was going to cry, and I guess I looked like it too, because he placed his hand on my shoulder and said, "Everything is going to be okay."

There was little question on the plane ride home about where we needed to have the surgery. Dr. Azizkhan was completely confident and reassuring that he could remove the tumor completely. However, there was not much hope, in his opinion, in saving the hipbone. He was fairly certain that full resection would require removing the bony structure surrounding the tumor. But if she had no hipbone, there would be no bony structure to support and power a prosthesis when she was old enough to walk. This was our dilemma. Do we take a chance on leaving a margin of tumor behind in hopes of leaving the hip joint so she could use a prosthesis later? Or do we remove all the bony structure, eliminating any residue of tumor, but also squelching any chance of using a prosthesis? It was a gut-wrenching decision.

When we had settled in back at home, I called our pastor for his advice. After relaying the information to him, Pastor Mike said, "It sounds like you already know what to do; you're just having a hard time saying it."

He nailed it. How would we tell our little girl one day that she couldn't have a prosthesis because we had made this decision for her? But how could we risk leaving the tumor behind? And how did I get to this place in my life where I had to make decisions like this? I did not feel qualified.

But before the next day, Scott and I both knew what had to be done. We called and talked with the scheduling assistant in Dr. Azizkhan's office, who told us the soonest we could schedule the surgery would be the first of December. We made a request that seems, from the outside, both immature and selfish: we asked if there was any way we could schedule the surgery before the first of November—before our basketball seasons started. In retrospect, I cannot believe it was even a factor for us. It seems petty and self-centered. But at the time, it was our livelihood and the only source of stability in our lives. Even now it sounds ridiculous. But God was working even through our immaturity. Sometimes, I have become increasingly convinced, God uses even our weaknesses, mistakes, and lack of experience to bring about His purposes.

The scheduling office called back to say there had been a cancellation and that, miraculously, they had been able to coordinate the schedules of all four surgeons involved for October 26. Would that work out for us?

Tryouts were the first full week in November. The timing could not have been better.

CHAPTER 10

JUST ONE STEP

Come to me all you who are weary and burdened and I will give you rest. Take my yoke upon you and learn from me, for I am gentle and humble in heart and you will find rest for your souls.

~ Matthew 11:28-29

WE HAD A FIRST BIRTHDAY party for Savannah the next weekend. We invited everybody we could think of who'd had some part in our lives over the last year and held the party outside on the back deck of our house that Scott's buddy Chris had helped him build that summer. Although being surrounded by the sight of all of the godsends in our lives, I couldn't shake the feeling of dread that lay over my shoulders like a heavy, wet coat. Watching Savannah dive face-first into her ladybug cake was a sweet moment of respite, but I was grieving privately over this next hurdle we'd have to jump.

We left for Cincinnati on Sunday, October 25. Our pastor was waiting when we arrived at the downtown airport to pray for us before we left. His son, Andrew, made the flight with us, and he wished us well as we loaded up our rental car and drove from the Cincinnati airport to the hospital. Our parents and sisters had already begun the drive to Ohio and would meet us at the hospital later that night.

After we had arrived and checked into the hospital, the doctors immediately ordered an MRI to check the tumor site one last time before surgery. Then we checked into a room and started the "cleansing" process—once again, a tube was placed down Savannah's nose and throat to start a drip that would clean out her colon before surgery. Oh, it was horrible. Though she couldn't tell me, the tube obviously hurt her throat, because her little voice was hoarse when she cried. It was miserable to watch.

Our family members stopped by one by one to visit and love on Savannah before the next morning. They also brought us goody bags from friends at church who had sent their best wishes along with their gifts to keep us occupied during the long hours we would be waiting over the next couple of days. Connie Harlow, the wife of our music minister, and her daughters Lisa and Lori sent a beautiful bag full of snacks, magazines, rolls of quarters for the vending machines, and stationery Connie had hand-painted herself. My mama brought me a pair of socks with monkeys on them. Monkeys crack me up, and she thought they might cheer me up a little. Little things . . .

As the evening wore on, the different surgeons stopped in to update us on the next morning's plan. The third doctor to stop by was a neurologist who wore a black leather biker's jacket. He pulled up a chair, and I could tell from the look on his face that this was not going to be good news. Dr. Myseros began to explain to us that the day's MRI showed that the tumor had indeed grown. It was now touching Savannah's spine. They wouldn't be able to tell how much of the spine was involved until they were in surgery. He wanted us to know that this would greatly complicate the surgery and posed an increased risk to Savannah. Depending on how deep the tumor had grown, removing the tumor could potentially cause paralysis.

When he finished talking and left us holding the weight of his words, I got up and left the room. I couldn't take anymore. I walked to the end of the hallway and looked out of the glass window into the jet black of night. I wasn't angry or crying or anything at all—I just couldn't take any more emotion.

My mother-in-law was in the room with us when the doctor came in, so she came out to check on me after a minute or two. I could see the reflection of her red fingernails in the window as she squeezed my shoulders and stood behind me for a long time. And I still feel really bad for being unable to reciprocate her affection and concern, but I just could not. I could not respond at all. I was frozen, afraid that if I showed just one tiny fragment of emotion, I would splinter into a million pieces. So I just stood there, rigid and silent and unresponsive until she left and went back to the room with Scott. I wish I could have let her love me, because I know that's all she was offering. But I just didn't want to feel anymore. I completely shut down.

I wonder if this is how soldiers survive war. I have heard stories about how difficult it is to show emotion when they return home because they have had to numb themselves for so long. Standing at the end of that hospital hallway, that's what I felt: numb. Hardened. But not through and through, just on the outside. Like a sculpture of tiny mosaic tiles held together by thin, watery glue—if one piece falls, the whole thing goes down with a crash. I knew I was teetering on a very frail trapeze line, and I didn't know what would happen if

I came crashing down at that moment. We hadn't even taken her to surgery yet.

I suddenly sensed a desperation rise up in me that I had never experienced before. And all at once, I dropped to my knees. Without emotion, without crying or drama or anything else, I surrendered. I gave up my last efforts to hold onto to any false hope of self-reliance. I was done. "I can't do this, Lord. I can't do it anymore. I need you to help us. You can have it all—my will, my pride, my life—but I need you to help me. I need to know who you are. You can have it all. I surrender. I surrender."

On my knees, alone at the end of a sterile hallway, the weight of the world began to fall off in pieces. I had the sense that chunks of armor were falling to the ground, heavy garments I had manufactured to protect my heart, to prove my self-reliance. I'd never realized how heavy my pride was, how hard it was to carry that armor around, how cumbersome, how confining. Surrendering to God was the lightest, most free I'd ever felt.

Those minutes at the end of that hallway separated the old from the new. I became something else that night. I had asked Jesus a long time ago to be my Savior, but that night I asked Him to be the Lord of my life. There's a difference. I had tried to hold that position all these years, to keep my independence and control over my own life. And now I realized it was just an illusion. I never really had it in the first place. That night, I turned over the deed to my life. I couldn't take the responsibility anymore. And something happened down deep: a lock broke, a chain fell, a prisoner was released. I know, it sounds dramatic and super-spiritual, but it couldn't have been less. It was a quiet, humble, simple moment between me and my Creator—a return of ownership to the one who owned it all to begin with. There were no pillars of fire, no flashing lights or voices in the dark—just a personal trip to the foot of the Cross where my life was paid for in full. I understood freedom for the first time. I didn't think I would walk back to the room to find all of our problems solved, but I suddenly felt real peace, that peace that transcends all understanding I had heard about all my life. His was a deep, true, pure peace that swallowed me up and gave me the strength to stand up and walk.

I don't know how long I stayed there at the end of the hall, and I wasn't sure what to expect after this encounter, but when I went back to the room, Scott was alone with Savannah. He was holding her by the bed and talking to her in a low, hushed voice while she held his gaze. Standing in the doorway, I couldn't hear the exact words he said to her, but I can imagine they were promises and reminders of God's faithfulness that would minister more to his heart than to the baby girl in his arms. But she didn't take her eyes off her daddy as he whispered to her. Her eyes were locked on his as tubes ran out of her nose and machines beeped. I almost turned and walked out, feeling like I was invading their precious and priceless moment. But Scott looked up at me just then, and he smiled at me in that way he has of saying, *It's going to be okay.*

This time, I decided to believe him. Because, really, what's the alternative? There have been so many times since then that people have said to one or both of us, "You were so strong during all of that," "Your faith was so strong," or "How did you do it?" I have to fight the urge to laugh out loud and say *Are you kidding me?* I don't know what people saw on the outside, but on the inside, what we *had* to do was believe she was going to make it. That was the only way for me to survive. I had to believe that this was going to turn out to be a happy ending. As Emily Dickinson penned from her attic bedroom, "Hope is the thing with feathers that perches in the soul." Our hearts were made for it. Without hope, we can't live. Not life in the way it was intended to be lived, anyway. So my answer to those kind people who somehow are mistaken into believing I was, of all things, faithful *or* strong during that time, I say, honestly, what's the alternative? I had a baby I was trying to keep alive and a husband who I knew, deep down, was as scared and broken as I was. So what were my options, really? I had to hold onto hope—had to believe that we'd make it through this. It's the choice we made: to hold onto hope instead of being swept up by the riptide of despair and hopelessness. There was no alternative, if we wanted our souls to stay alive.

We decided that, since there was only one fold-out chair in the hospital room, I would stay with Savannah through the night and Scott would sleep at the hotel. After he kissed us both good night, he left for a few hours of sleep before meeting us back in the room at 5 a.m. I changed us both into sleep clothes. Hers was a snuggly cream-colored footed-pajama with Winnie the Pooh and the words "it's the SMALLISH things in life that take up the most room in our hearts" embroidered on the front. I placed Savannah in my lap, trying to keep from tangling us both in the tubes running from her nose to the IV drip hanging above her crib. I opened up a bag I had brought from home filled with books and toys she liked, and pulled out one of our favorite books called *Hermie the Common Caterpillar* by Max Lucado. It's a precious and beautiful story about a plain green caterpillar who wants to look like all the other colorful and talented creatures around him: the ladybug with the beautiful spots, the ant who flaunts his strength by carrying a pine cone 100 times his size, the snail who wears his own house on his back. Day after day, Hermie goes to God to ask him why he made him so ordinary. And each time, God answers him with, "Because I love you, Hermie, and I'm not finished with you yet."

To this day, every time I read the story, I get choked up. But on that night, I was a puddle of a woman. Little Savannah, a snuggly pooh bear herself, was settling down in my lap as she helped me turn the pages, but I was beginning to unravel. In the end of the story, Hermie falls asleep—and awakens to total and terrifying darkness. But as he tries to squirm, the darkness around him begins to crack, and he feels a "tickle" on his back as the cocoon falls away. Hermie's darkness is replaced by beautiful, fluttering wings that take him to soaring heights and sweeping views. I began to cry hard, saying over and over to God, "You can't be finished with her yet. I know you're not finished with her yet. She's barely a year old. You just can't be finished with her yet."

Around eleven o'clock, just as Savannah finally fell asleep, a nurse came in to check the "cleansing" progress. She woke up my dreaming princess, much to my irritation. Savannah's little bottom was red and raw from so much diaper changing, but the diaper still wasn't "clear" and the order was given for an enema. By the time the enema supplies arrived around midnight, Savannah's backside was actually bleeding, and she screamed in pain as the nurse administered the enema. I was mad and all but yelling at the nurse that this was horrible and that there was no reason to do this to a baby.

She finally turned to me and said, "Mrs. Duke, I don't enjoy doing this, but she can't go into surgery until her bowels are clean. The doctors won't risk getting any bacteria in the surgery site, so I'm just trying to help you be ready for the surgery in the morning. If you want me to stop, I will, but I can't guarantee she'll be able to have the operation tomorrow if you don't let me clean her out."

Calmed only slightly, I stopped yelling at her, and I walked around to the other side of the crib where Savannah's face was. I laid mine down next to hers and cried with her as I tried to comfort her. When it was over, the nurse left us alone, both of us crying. Savannah's voice was barely audible now, completely hoarse from the tube still draining in her throat and from all the crying we were doing together. She was exhausted and fell asleep almost as soon as I began rocking her. I rocked her until I couldn't stay awake anymore and only laid her in her crib because I was afraid I might drop her if I fell asleep. We both slept fitfully.

My mama woke me before the sun was up. She came in quietly around 4:30 and I took a much needed shower there in the room while she rocked and held her grandbaby. When I came out of the bathroom, Scott had arrived and the nurse was checking her diaper one last time. It was finally clean.

By 5:15 a.m., when the OR nurse came for us, the rest of our family had arrived. They followed us to the operating wing of the hospital. Scott carried Savannah in his right arm, and she played peek-a-boo over his shoulder at the people who loved her more than anybody else in the world. Just before we reached the area where only Scott and I were allowed to carry her, as her extended family waved and said their good-byes, she brought the house down as she blew them all a tiny kiss with homecoming queen flair.

Scott and I held her for a few minutes back in the OR area until the doctors arrived, and then it was time to hand off our baby one last time. We had to physically hand over her little thirteen-month old life—and the epicenter of *our* life—to a stranger wearing a paper shower cap and pajamas. Scott had to pry her from my arms, and she blew us more kisses on her way through the swinging doors.

I wiped the tears away as fast as they fell, trying to retain some shred of composure, really just enough to keep my feet moving forward as we were led yet again to a small waiting room. A nurse told us the doctor would meet with us periodically during the surgery to keep us updated on the progress, and then she left us there in that tiny closet of a room for a few minutes of privacy before beginning the long wait with our family.

When the door shut behind her, Scott and I fell apart all over each other and began to cry and pray all at the same time. With his voice breaking and overcome with sobs, Scott said some things I had never thought about before. He said, "I love that little girl now. I didn't really *know* her the first time she had surgery—she wasn't really old enough to have much of a personality. But now, now I know her—her personality, her expressions, the way her face lights up when I walk in the room. I can't stand the thought of losing her now." For the first time, kneeling there with my arms wrapped around him with his hands over his face in that little waiting room, I saw his own personal crisis laid bare before me. This was not just my tragedy. It was his too. He had always been the strong one, the glue that held the pieces of me together. But it was my turn to hold him. I saw his pain that morning, his human-ness and the frailness of a father's heart as we waited helplessly while our baby slept under the surgeon's knife.

CHAPTER 11

WHILE WE WAIT

Do not fear, for I have redeemed you; I have summoned you
by name; you are mine. When you pass through the waters, I
will be with you; and when you pass through the rivers, they
will not sweep over you. When you walk through the fire,
you will not be burned; the flames will not set you ablaze. For
I am the LORD your God, the Holy One of Israel, your Savior.

~ Isaiah 43:1b–3

LIKE MOST CIRCUMSTANCES IN OUR life, my husband and I are
on opposite ends of the spectrum in how we deal with stress. Our
waiting room strategies couldn't have been more different. Scott
planted himself right smack in the middle of our families, flanked by
board games and puzzles to help pass the time. I, on the other hand,
wedged myself into a hole in the wall—a tiny nook in between wall
studs in the corner of the waiting room section where our families
had set up camp. I had packed bags loaded with photos and scrapbook
supplies, armed with the tools I needed to record Savannah's first
year of life for posterity. I had no desire to take my mind off of what
was going on in the adjoining room. I didn't feel like laughing and

playing games and pretending like this all wasn't happening, though it probably would have been better for all of us. Instead, I channeled all of my attention and energy into completing a scrapbook celebrating my daughter and recording all of the happy and blessed moments we had lived since she was born. I also didn't want everybody's eyes on me, trying to determine if I was okay or not, asking me if I needed anything. I just wanted to be left alone.

I knew it was selfish. They needed me as much as I needed them. Waiting rooms are holding cells of torment, psychological torture chambers for family members holding their breath for a good report. No one sitting in a waiting room actually wants to be there. Our very presence indicates some level of calamity. But the waiting room also gives opportunity for loved ones to come alongside, a rally point to shoulder each other and shoo away fearsome thoughts. To say things like, "She's a tough little cookie. She's gonna do great."

But my mind couldn't gloss over what was going on in that operation room. I kept wondering what instrument the doctor was holding at the moment. Call me morbid, but I felt compelled to pray over every minute of the surgery, to imagine each part of the process and ask God to cover it. As much as I loved my family, I needed to do this in my way—and I didn't want to talk. So, I holed up in my cocoon and began to work on Savannah's scrapbook. (Yes, to all my scrapbook sisters and fellow creative junkies, this is where it all began.) In between updates from the doctors, I spent the day cutting and pasting and journaling and laughing and crying and documenting my daughter's life while I prayed.

A few hours into the operation, Dr. Myseros, the neurosurgeon who had come the night before to explain the involvement of the spine, sent word for us to meet him in the small conference room where Scott and I had started the day. My stomach lurched.

We hurried to the conference room, and he met us with a smile. He said what they had believed was tumor on the spine turned out to be a small cyst that was removed easily and without any apparent damage. He wanted, however, to check her sensation and reflexes later in the week after she had had a chance to recover, but he was confident that her spine and nerves had been spared. He patted us both on the shoulder and said not to worry: Dr. Azizkhan was the best. I grabbed him and hugged him, and he just smiled and let me.

Scott updated our families, and I went back to my hole. I laid my Bible out on the floor in front of me and wrote a promise from his Word on every page of the scrapbook. Pictures of her first ultrasound accented with Psalm 139; photos from Greenville Hospital inscribed with Isaiah 43:1–3 and 40:13:, Savannah asleep on my chest with Matthew 11:29 written beneath—snapshots of her life, all underscored with a verse of Scripture that gave me new perspective to the images caught on film. Every page I finished became a marker of how far God had brought us. Every page gave me renewed faith and courage that we were being held.

The waiting room became a revolving door. One by one, each family of patients set up camp to carry out their tour of duty until the receptionist called for the family of so-and-so and the doctor gave the good news that all is right in the world, or not. Although somber, the waiting chamber was a constant coming and going—like an airport where groups wait for the call for their plane to board, gather their belongings, and then take off for their destination. After the doctor's report, each waiting room family spoke words of relief or encouragement to each other as they packed up and left, and a new family soon came in to begin their shift.

Person after person, family after family, group after group came and went that Friday, and we watched them all. At 6 a.m., we were the first family in the waiting room, and at 5 p.m. we watched the next to the last family leave. We knew it would be a long day. Dr. Azizkhan estimated the operation would take nine or ten hours. But every time a family name was called and it was evident that someone's beloved had made it to the recovery room, we all stopped and watched quietly: a silent envy held all of our eyes on the freed captives, watching their relief and wishing for the same. We were all tired—suffering from lack of sleep, lack of substantial food, and lack of patience. Everybody was tired of playing Trivial Pursuit, I was out of pictures, all the stories had been told, and we wanted this to be over.

We were a weary bunch, pensive and ragged, when Dr. Azizkhan walked in at 6 p.m. We all stood, and Scott and I scrambled to meet him halfway. He was smiling.

"She came through beautifully," he said, and I threw my arms around his neck like he was my long-lost father. Now, I'm not an extremely affectionate person, so it surprised me as much as it did him, but I just couldn't help myself. It was an eruption of relief and tension and joy that I just didn't have the strength to suppress at that moment. And although I doubt he was expecting me to throw myself upon him, he hugged me back anyway. I cried. And Dr. Azizkhan just stood and hugged me until I could pull away and stand up straight, thus dispelling the rumor that good doctors must be cool and detached.

With our family standing around us in a semi-circle, Dr. Azizkhan explained all the different parts of the surgery: the orthopedist's removal of the hip and pelvis, the size of the tumor wrapped around the femur as they lifted it out, the accomplishments of the urologist and gynecologist who attended to the long-term details. Although the tumor was roughly a quarter of her body weight, miraculously, he said, there had been no damage to any of her organs as far as they could tell. He wouldn't know for certain until later, of course, but the tumor had separated from all of the surrounding organs and inner parts with ease and without any apparent damage.

"It took longer than we thought, but we are confident that we have removed all margins of the tumor. It was significantly larger than we thought it would be. The fact that we removed it without severe damage to any organs is nothing short of, well, a miracle." He paused and looked around at all of us. "You all must be people of faith," he said with a smile.

We all nodded in unison. I could hear sniffles behind me, but no one said a word. None of us could speak.

Before he left, he stepped forward and hugged each of us. When he turned and walked away, still stately and gracious after thirteen hours in the OR, we all just stood there, stunned. It was over. The tumor was gone. Slowly, we began to hug each other, the heaviness of the day settling into our bones. It was finally our turn to mumble the words of relief, pack our belongings, and scurry to the recovery room to see our baby girl.

We were corralled in the hallway outside the children's ICU waiting for the nursing staff to bring in Savannah from the OR. All of us were trying to prepare each other emotionally for what she would look like. We knew she would be swollen and hooked to lots of tubes, but when the nurse came out to let me and Scott in to see her, I was not prepared for the toil her little body had taken.

Similar to the surgery at Duke, she had little rectangular patches of raw skin from the tape that held the breathing tubes in place during the surgery. The fluids she had been given during the operation had made her swell so much that she looked like she might pop. But she was beautiful and alive, and I rubbed her hand as she slept and whispered in her ear how much we loved her. We let our family see her two by two, and Scott and I were allowed to stay in a parent sleeping room overnight since she'd just come out of surgery. We said good night to our families and slept hard on an uncomfortable cot made for one but sufficient for the both of us on this night. The weight of the world lifted as we succumbed to sleep.

Early the next morning, we found her awake and charming the nurses in the ICU. Although still attached to an IV and healing from the day before, she was smiling and held her hands out for us to hold her. We each gingerly maneuvered around the wires and tubes that monitored her; we held her gently in turn. Within the hour, the doctor decided she was strong enough to be taken to the children's ward, where she would spend the next five to seven days recovering and healing from the surgery. Our families had arrived and so we all migrated to the adjoining wing of the hospital, shuffling along in a herd like a nomadic tribe following their warrior princess.

When she was settled in her new room and had been given her pain medication, my parents and sisters decided it was probably time for them to go back home to South Carolina and give us space by ourselves with our baby. Scott and I were so grateful for their support, and I wanted to walk them out, so Scott suggested I take them down to the cafeteria for breakfast. My sister Heather, who is the pickiest eater I've ever known, decided she'd skip breakfast and spend the time with Savannah instead, so I walked down with my parents and sister Jenny to the cafeteria on the first floor. I hadn't eaten anything substantial in several days, so I loaded up with all of my favorite breakfast foods, and we all sat down to the best meal I could remember in a long time.

About halfway through my breakfast, Heather walked up to the table looking ill. "Hey, Wendy," she said, breathless, "Scott needs you to come upstairs."

"Okay," I said, thinking the doctor must be coming up to meet with us. "Are you okay?" I asked, noticing how pale she seemed.

"Yeah, yeah," Heather answered. "He just needs you *right* now."

"Okay—"

I left my food on the table and started out of the cafeteria toward the elevators down the hall. Then the switch flipped, and I knew something was wrong. Panic flooded and I started to sprint down the hall, bumping into people and not caring because I knew something was very wrong. I banged on the elevator button until the doors opened, and I prayed all the way to the fourth floor that they were okay. I ran around the corner of the hall and saw Scott holding Savannah in his arms over her bed, his face white as a sheet, a flurry of nurses swarming them.

"What happened?!" I said from the hallway, which seemed to get longer and longer as I made my way to the room. My legs were moving as if in deep water. I made it to where they stood and realized that Scott was shaking. I thought he might be sick.

"She stopped breathing," he said quietly as several nurses checked monitors.

"What, why? What *happened?*" I asked again, slinging my arms around them both.

"She stopped breathing. She was blue." Scott spoke in this weird, strange voice I'd never heard before. He held onto Savannah like he was never letting go, and she just blinked up at him without moving.

"Her oxygen rate is up," one nurse said to the other hurriedly, moving things around and checking charts and monitors. "I think she's okay now, but we've called the doctor, and he's ordered us to take her off the morphine to make sure it doesn't happen again."

"Do you know why this happened?" I asked the nurse.

She told us the morphine they had given Savannah to control pain sometimes depresses the lungs, causing the oxygen levels to drop dramatically. Savannah's had dropped too low. "Her lungs went to sleep." She assured me they had administered an antidote to reverse the effects of the morphine and she should be fine, but they wanted to watch her very carefully.

Scott handed me our baby girl and sank into the rocking chair by the bed, still shaking. "I was just standing here holding her and talking to Heather when all these bells started going off and everybody came rushing in here. They grabbed her and were trying to give her oxygen but the number on the monitor kept dropping. Wendy," he looked up at me, "she was turning blue. She was *blue,* and there was nothing I could do. The number kept dropping and dropping and dropping and she was blue. Somebody came in with some kind of injection and the numbers started coming back up, but there was nothing I could do. There was nothing I could do . . ."

The nurse took Savannah to her crib to check vitals again, and I went over and knelt down in front of Scott, wrapping my arms around him. I had never seen him so shaken. "Of course there was nothing you could do, baby. There was nothing anybody could do."

The nurse was still checking and moving and making me nervous, but she finally seemed satisfied that Savannah's oxygen level was stable, and she gave her some Tylenol to manage pain. For the rest of the week, our one-year old had nothing stronger than Tylenol to manage the pain from a twelve-hour surgery. I had already popped four Advil that morning.

Our families all left for home that afternoon, and we spent the next couple of days waiting for our baby girl to recover. After the morphine incident, we were both a little more on edge than usual and constantly checked all of the monitors surrounding her bed. She was obviously sore, and holding her seemed to be very uncomfortable for her, so we were afraid to pick her up very much. So, most of those days, one or both of us would lie down next to her and read to her or sing songs. I can't remember her crying even once. She just watched us with her sweet blue-green eyes gazing up into our faces or studying the pictures in the books we read her. Not a sound did she make.

And then on the third day, she woke us up with little smacking noises. I jumped up off the fold-out chair to find out what was making the noise, and then I saw her: her little round face was filled with a grin from ear to ear and she was smacking her lips together, blowing us kisses. We lay on each side of her and wiped tears of joy from our faces, relieved to have our little girl back.

Mid-week, the surgeon who had removed the cyst from her spine came in to test for any nerve damage to her lower body and leg. He held a long metal instrument in front of her foot. We all held our breath as he touched the metal tip to her heel. For a few seconds, time seemed to stand still. He touched it again. And then she kicked him square in the nose.

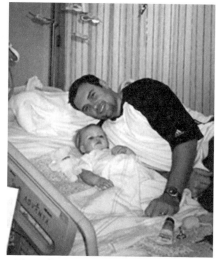

All smiles, two days after surgery

"Well," he said with a laugh, rubbing his nose and smiling, "She definitely has full use of her leg." I think he was just as relieved as we were.

The rest of the week went by without incident. We took turns sleeping at the hotel so that at least one of us got a good night's sleep each day. I worked on my scrapbook everyday—pictures and papers spread out on a rolling cart I had set up as my work station. One of the nurses on the hall brought me some scrapbooking idea books and let me look through her own family scrapbook. One afternoon, a resident medical student came by to check on Savannah and saw one of my layouts on the table.

"Is this what her leg looked like at birth?" he asked.

"Yes, this is the day she was born. That's the tumor there on the back of the leg." I pointed out the close-ups of the monster we had slain a few days earlier. "We hope we're past all this now and can move on."

"Would you mind if I borrowed this photo for a few hours?" the med student asked. "We have a seminar this afternoon, and I think this would be very interesting to the doctors who will be there. We were just discussing your daughter yesterday, and no one has ever heard of this kind of a teratoma having this degree of complications on a patient of her age. I'd just like for them to be able to see it in its original state."

"Sure." He thanked me and returned the pictures the next morning. To this day, I have no idea what resulted from the seminar, but I prayed they would see something in my baby's first pictures that would help someone else someday.

By Friday, we were tired and anxious to take our little girl home. She was recovering well and gaining back her strength and bubbly personality. That afternoon, Dr. Azizkhan stopped by with one of the hospital's oncologists. They had just received the biopsy report.

"Good news, Dukes. It appears that we have removed all the margins of the tumor. But it's a good thing we removed it when we did. It was encapsulated within the tumor, but it had begun to metastasize— to break down. If we had waited even one more week, the cancer could have spread to other parts of her body. The timing couldn't have been more crucial."

Dr. Azizkhan gave us the green light to check out later that night after his evening rounds. He asked us to stay in town over the weekend and come in for a follow-up appointment in his office on Monday, but he didn't see any reason why we couldn't check out of the hospital and all get a good night's sleep, all in one place.

"You've got one strong little girl here," he said before he signed the necessary paperwork and left the room.

We sat there quietly for a few minutes, both of us thinking the same thing: the only reason we scheduled this surgery now instead of December was so that we wouldn't miss too much of our basketball seasons. It had seemed so self-serving and petty at the time, but if we'd not had teams to manage in early November—the following week, to be exact—we would have waited another six weeks and that might have been too late. The weight of that thought fell heavy on us, and we didn't talk about it then, but we have since discussed how God's omniscience and perfect timing manifested itself in the busyness of our schedules. In a crazy way—orchestrated by a God who is big enough to pull off something like this—basketball saved our daughter's life.

After some last-minute testing and checking and making sure all was well, Dr. Azizkhan released us from the hospital that night. We spent the weekend with Scott's friend Shane and felt like released prisoners. Having our baby in the fresh air was a gift. We took her to the Cincinnati Zoo on Saturday, perched in her stroller like the Princess and the Pea on top of a pile of blankets to cushion her healing backside. As would become her trademark, she watched every animal closely before deciding whether or not she wanted to get closer. We had a blast. It was a glorious day—one of the highlights in my memory.

We checked into Dr. Azizkhan's office Monday morning, and ironically, only had to wait about five minutes before we were called back to his office for Savannah to receive a clean bill of health. Dr. Azizkhan hugged us all, and we posed for a picture with him and his nursing staff. It's one of my favorites.

Dr. Azizkhan and staff at Cincinnati
Children's, a week after surgery

We flew home a week and a half after we'd arrived in Cincinnati. I rode in the back of the small aircraft holding my sleeping baby, wrapped in her favorite blanket covered with tiny red hearts, and reflected on the events of the last ten days. A story kept coming to mind—the story of Shadrach, Meshach, and Abednego tied up and thrown into a wicked king's fire. As the king looked into the blazing furnace, he saw not only the three men "unbound and unharmed" but also a fourth who looked "like a son of the gods." The text of Daniel 3 goes on to say that when the king called for the men to come out of the blazing furnace, "the fire had not harmed their bodies, nor was a hair of their heads singed; their robes were not scorched, and there was no smell of fire on them" (verse 27).

Looking back at our fiery furnace, I could clearly see the Son of God standing by our side, enduring the heat with us. Savannah had come out of that surgery without a hair being scorched, and our hearts were not burned up in the process. But I recognized that something else had happened to me personally: I had been unbound. The ropes of my own personal captivity—my pride, my inability to depend on God completely, my need and desire to have control—those were the only things that were burned away in the fire. Something deep in me had been set free in that furnace. And my life has never been the same.

I hope that those who look in at our story, at our journey through the fire, see not just the three of us but also the Son of God standing with us, shielding us from the flames. Instead of burning us up, this fire refined us, burned away the impurities, and brought out what is true and pure. We learned what is really important. We learned that God is fully, completely, always trustworthy; that He can move mountains, save us from our circumstances and ourselves. And I learned that my life and the lives of those I love are much safer in His hands than in mine.

I hope you'll see in our furnace the presence of the one true God, who is mighty to save and has no greater desire than to be known by His children. I know Him now. I cringe to think of how little I knew of God when life was easy. I can praise Him in a way I couldn't before. And I am overwhelmed with gratefulness at how, in His patience and completely undeserved mercy, He has shown up for me time and time again.

And He can do it for you too.

CHAPTER 12

ON THE WATER

Shortly before dawn Jesus went out to them, walking on
the lake. When the disciples saw him walking on the lake,
they were terrified. "It's a ghost," they said, and cried out
in fear.

But Jesus immediately said to them: "Take courage! It is I.
Don't be afraid."

"Lord, if it's you," Peter replied, "tell me to come to you on
the water."

"Come," he said. Then Peter got down out of the boat, walked
on the water and came toward Jesus.

But when he saw the wind, he was afraid and, beginning to
sink, cried out, "Lord, save me!"

Immediately Jesus reached out his hand and caught him.
"You of little faith," he said, "why did you doubt?"

~ Matthew 14:22–30

THE GUN FIRED AND I calmly watched her execute a *pretty impres-
sive* entry dive, if I do say so myself. There were only three little girls
in this event. Most of the crowd had come to see the older kids swim
in the more competitive races that would follow. But as I watched

my daughter pump her little arms wildly, I realized she was *in the lead,* and my heart started thumping in my neck. She had finished last in all but one race so far, but this time she was out in front at the halfway mark.

Okay, so I need to confess that I had watched the other mothers at these swim meets, yelling insanely and jumping up and down as if this were the actual Olympics. I thought it was silly, ridiculous behavior for grown men and women. They were six-year-olds, for cryin' out loud.

But that was before my kid had ever been in the lead, and at the present moment I was up on my feet, and my heart was racing as the enemy first-grader with pigtails in the lane next to her started to close in.

"GO-O-O-O, Savannah!!!" I screamed like a banshee, forming a megaphone with my hands and elbowing people out of the way as I edged toward the finish line. I hadn't experienced that kind of adrenaline rush since my coaching days. *"You can do it, baby!"* I screamed, and one of her little teammates joined in, "You can do it, Savannah!"

Some of the other parents and teammates began to notice, and soon most of the spectators were on their feet, yelling, "Go, Savannah! You can do it!" as the swimmers kicked and stroked and thrashed the final few yards.

The insanity of motherhood overpowered my sensibilities, and I leaped in the air, pumping my fists, when she reached out and touched the side of the pool. *She won! She won!* I zeroed in on her goggle-covered face to watch her reaction. She looked around in her pink goggles and saw the other little girls finishing *after* her, and her expression was more of surprise than excitement. I was practically knocking people into the pool trying to get to her, and when I reached the side of the pool, she said, "Hey, Mama! I think I got first place!"

"I know, baby, I *saw* you!" I said as I swooped her up into a hug. I hug her after every race and tell her how proud I am of her, even when she finishes last, because every word is true. I can't express how my heart swells every time she swims the length of that pool, not because it's a race but because she is a living, breathing, *swimming* testimony of God's wonder and power. Because she has overcome so much. Because she works so hard and congratulates her own team-mates even when she finishes last. Because she is a fighter.

But in all the excitement, I forgot to bring her towel. So when I wrapped my arms around her, she said, "Mama! Your clothes are get-ting all wet, silly!"

I didn't care. I just held on and kissed the top of her wet head. Because that's what crazy, adrenaline-laced, screaming, obnoxiously proud Mama Bears do.

Since October of 2001, when we had our last major surgery, we've slowly but surely learned how to live out a different kind of normal. We had a small follow-up surgery a few months after Cincinnati, but it was a breeze in comparison to the others. When she was almost two, Savannah got her first walker through the awesome people at the Shriner's Hospital here in Greenville. It had a little basket

Navigating the walker, 20 months old

for carrying toys on the front, and a horn that announced she was coming through.

First full family photo with her new baby brother, 2003

Her baby brother was born when she was two and a half, so she had to learn to share her toys and attention. Lots of people have asked me if I was scared during my pregnancy with my son—was I afraid we would have complications or health problems again? And I have to say that I really wasn't. I know it sounds cliché, or maybe I'm just ridiculously naïve, but I honestly learned, through our trials with Savannah, that God could be trusted, so it wasn't hard to do again. I don't really deal with fear much anymore. When you've looked death square in the face, little else seems very scary.

My pregnancy with our son was as smooth and uneventful as we could ask for, and Savannah was thrilled to have a baby brother. (Turns out, maybe I should have had a little healthy fear over having a second child, because that boy was a holy terror of a baby.) But JP completed our family and keeps things interesting around here. When he was three, he took a flying leap off our unfinished deck into the arms of his daddy, fifteen feet below. He said he knew Daddy would catch him, and I knew we were in big trouble. That same summer he jumped into the deep end of the pool without knowing how to swim—twice. I ruined two cell phones and a key fob diving in after him.

I think he was five before he realized that his sister only had one leg and that other people had two. He still calls her "Sissy," even though he's eleven and four inches taller than she, which brings her no end of irritation. Siblings have a way of keeping us from thinking too highly of ourselves or living under the illusion that we will always get our way.

Adventurous, fearless, and protective, he is a fantastic brother to his big sister. He regularly carries her lunchbox or her book-bag; sometimes he'll even carry her on his back if they have to walk an especially long way. But he's had to figure out how to live in the shadow of his older sister, which I guess all second children have to do—but that girl casts a pretty big shadow. So he's finding his own way, and God has his own plan for that one, the one with the big, servant's heart who looks out for others and leaps from the scariest heights. God is already working in his life.

Savannah graduated to straight-arm crutches when she was three, a coordination of body parts and metal that made me a nervous wreck until she got the hang of them. Now other kids find them fascinating and pretend to walk on them, or use them as imaginary guns.

Walking will always take her some extra effort, but swimming has always been perfectly natural to Savannah. She loved the water from the first summer we spent in my parents' pool, and she learned to swim when she was about three. *The Little Mermaid* was her favorite movie, and we couldn't keep her out of the water. It was the one place where she was on equal footing. So when she wanted to join the neighborhood swim team at age six, we didn't have a hard time saying yes. Little JP followed her lead and joined with her. He's since lost interest and moved to other sports, but that first swim season was just the beginning of a love of athletics and competition.

When our children are babies, we imagine all sorts of good things for them. Their first birthday, their first bike ride, their first home run. Their first game-winning shot or first solo in choir. I had never been involved in swimming and can barely tread water myself, so swim meets was not something I ever envisioned for my children. But, this script is constantly evolving, and nobody's exactly asking me for suggestions. And who am I to put limitations on what might be possible for my children? Savannah has amazed me at what she is able to do, despite being an amputee and cancer survivor. I can't say I *always* swell with pride when I look at her—especially when I've caught her smacking her little brother or painting the walls with my lipstick—but almost every time.

But I've *never* been more proud than a year or so before that eventful swim meet, when Savannah took a dive into another kind of pool—one that would bestow on her more than a blue ribbon, but a crown in heaven instead.

A few months after Savannah turned five, she began to ask me and Scott about baptism. What was it? Why did people do it? Could she be baptized? We explained to her that being baptized is something that people do to let other people know that they asked Jesus to come and live in their hearts—to let people know we follow Jesus. Pretty soon, she began to ask us every night if she could ask Jesus into her heart. My husband and I would go to bed debating the issue each night. He thought she was ready. Frankly, I thought she was way too young to grasp all that being a Christian would entail. How could a five-year-old child possibly understand what following Jesus would cost her?

But it's the first step that matters most. Sometimes, we just have to take the first step, and the others will fall into place. Once again,

I had missed the main idea for the details. Once again, I had confused knowledge for wisdom. Once again, I had made the means to Jesus much more important than the Savior himself. I finally told Savannah that we would ask Pastor Doug, our children's pastor, what he thought. And so night after night, Savannah would ask if we could go to Pastor Doug's office the next day. And night after night, I would have some reason why we couldn't, something we just *had* to do instead.

On Christmas Day, 2005—a Sunday morning that year—I went to pick up Savannah from children's church after the service, and she practically dragged me to the bathroom. I thought she needed help, but when I closed the door and turned around, she was standing so close I almost knocked her down.

"What do you need, honey?" I knelt down and asked.

"Mama, I want to tell Pastor Doug that I asked Jesus into my heart. Can you go with me?"

"Baby, you can't tell him that until after you *have* asked Jesus into your heart."

"*Mama*," she said in a tone that sounded more like *Knucklehead*, "I already did. I asked him into my heart last night in my bed because I got tired of waiting on you guys. He already lives here," she said as she tapped the middle of her chest.

Although this was not my finest parenting moment, it was a reminder that God can speak clearly to a child's heart without a middle man. I had been so worried about making sure she understood the weight of this decision that I missed the chance to be a part of my daughter's first experience with the Living God. But he didn't miss it. I guess they just needed me to introduce them, but he had it from there. He had been pursuing her, and she had reached out her hand to accept His proposal without needing my permission.

I hoped this was not foreshadowing of her teenage years.

I followed her out the door of the bathroom feeling a little like a guilty child who had been shown mercy as she walked up to Pastor Doug and asked if she could tell him something. I'll never forget the image of him kneeling down to look her in the eyes, and how his eyes filled with tears as she shared with him the news she wanted to tell him. He looked up to me, and I just shook my head and said, "This was all her. I can't take any credit for it."

Pastor Doug prayed with Savannah and then told her he wanted to talk with her and her mama and daddy in his office. So we made an appointment to see him a few weeks later, where he sat in the floor with her and asked her question after question about why Jesus had to die and why she needed Him to live in her heart. When she said she needed Jesus to clean out her heart from all her sin and help her not to hurt God's feelings anymore, it was all I could do not to weep aloud. To think that even her small acts of disobedience and sin toward her brother grieved her heart that much spoke conviction into my own heart.

After a thorough interview, Doug took me aside and said, "She's got it. She's got a better grasp of what following Jesus means than many adults I know. She's ready." And so we all walked downstairs to the stairwell where Isaiah 49:16 is painted on the wall: *I will not forget you! See, I have engraved you on the palms of my hands."*

Pastor Doug then dipped Savannah's hand in red paint and helped her place her handprint on the wall among other handprints of assorted sizes and colors. They wrote her name and the date beneath it, and then he prayed with Savannah there below her handprint. It is one of my favorite memories.

As we started to leave to go home, Savannah asked if she had to be baptized now. Pastor Doug explained to her that being baptized doesn't save us from our sins, but it's like wearing a jersey to show we're part of the team. It's like telling Jesus we're proud to be a part of His family. Assessing the look on her face, Doug told her she could wait as long as she wanted until she was ready to be baptized. So Savannah made the decision to wait.

At Easter, our choir held a Good Friday service at our church, a musical drama about the days leading up to the crucifixion and burial of Christ. My husband was playing the part of the apostle John, and I was singing in the choir, but Savannah wanted to see the "show" about Jesus, so she sat with my mother during the service. It was a very moving production. After the crucifixion scene, the apostles carried Jesus' body through the sanctuary toward the "tomb" in the choir loft. Scott was moved to tears as he carried the body right past the seat where Savannah sat crying. The service ended quietly as Jesus' body was placed in the tomb and the disciples went their separate ways to grieve their loss. The crowd exited the sanctuary in silence.

No one talked much as we hung our choir robes on their hangers. It was the most somber event I've ever experienced—moving and emotional for everyone. As I walked pensively through the hallway toward the nursery to pick up JP, our three year old, Savannah barreled into me on her crutches, sobbing hysterically. "Mama, why did they have to be so mean to Him? Why were they so *mean* to Jesus?" she pleaded between sobs. I knelt down and held her tightly and fought to compose myself before I finally said, "Baby, we were worth all of that to Jesus. He would have done that all over again just for you, because He loves you and me so much. We were worth it to Him, baby. We were worth it to Him."

And we stayed like that for a long time. Then Savannah did something I will never forget as long as I live. She stood up straight, wiped the tears from her face with the back of her hand, and said, "I want to be baptized now. Even though I'm scared, I want Jesus to know He's worth it to me too."

On Sunday night, May 13, 2006, I helped Savannah change into a white robe outside the baptism pool. Her daddy would do the honors. We had been serving in ministry for the last three years, and our pastor asked Scott if he wanted the privilege of baptizing our daughter. That's not an opportunity to pass up.

As the service started, I stood on the opposite side of the baptism pool to make sure I had a clear view (not to mention a clear camera shot for this obvious scrapbook moment). Our church has a tradition of giving family and friends, or anyone who had a part of the new believer coming to know the Lord, the opportunity to stand in support of their brother or sister in Christ. As our pastor announced that Savannah Duke would be baptized by her father, the whole congregation stood to their feet when they entered the water. Our church family had walked this road with us. They had "stood before God in the gap on our behalf" like Ezekiel, supporting us in prayer during the darkest days; they had "stood shoulder to shoulder with us" like Isaiah, carrying much of our burdens through Savannah's trials; and they were now standing alongside us as she took a stand for her Savior, her Hero.

With his voice breaking, Scott asked Savannah if she had asked Jesus to be her Lord and Savior. She proudly answered, "Yes, sir!" and her daddy leaned her back beneath the clear water. The whole church applauded as she rose out of the water, officially following in Jesus' footsteps. It was a humbling moment.

There's something about water that brings a sense of vitality, renewal, freshness, cleansing. It's the reason I have to start the day with a shower. I need that invigorating cleansing from all of the weight of the day before and the heaviness of the last six or seven hours of sleep. Water has always symbolized life—it's the metaphor used throughout literature to represent the moving, swelling constant force. Physically, we can't live without it. Jesus personified Himself as "the living water" (John 4:13–14). We can't have the abundant life He promises us without Him (John 10:10). Without water, life ceases to exist.

For me, that sense of being alive is different now. For as long as I can remember, I have always had dreams about being underwater. I would be deep beneath the water's surface panicking, holding my breath long enough to make it to the air above. Each time, I would feel my lungs begin to burn and then almost burst as I frantically tried to find the surface. And finally, in spite of my battling, I would take in a gigantic breath of water—surely the kiss of death. I have always feared drowning, and surely this is how it begins. But in my dreams, as my lungs filled with water, contrary to my fears, I took in the water easily and smoothly—as if the water was what I should have been inhaling and exhaling all along. Somehow, my lungs were made to breathe this substance, and it was far better than the smog and smoke that air seemed like now. Was this possible? This is crazy—we can't breathe underwater. And yet in those dreams I would swim through the water like an eagle in the air—soaring through the currents as if I were made for this. Flowing, floating, powered along by this new life source.

I would inevitably wake up, disappointed to be above water.

In many ways, my life has been this way. In the waves that crashed around us and threatened to drown the life of my little girl, as I battled to get out of that water and back to the surface of life, I was forced to take a big gulp of The Living Water. And I survived. Not only survived, but found real life. The only breath that kept me alive was His. And I want to stay so close that I breathe Him in every moment.

Okay, sometimes I get a really big breath of Him and try to go off and swim my own way for a while—but it doesn't take me long to recognize I'm too far from the shore so that I hurry to come back to Him and be revived. But I've found it much more invigorating (and less frantic) to stay close, moment by moment, day by day. And by staying close and recognizing the power of His living water, I am freed from the heavy burden of trying to swim against the current of this world on my own, holding my breath all the way.

Scott and I have been forever changed by God's provision for our family during that dark storm. Our lives have been affected in a way that only God could orchestrate.

In 2003, Scott sensed that still, small voice of God calling us to serve him in a full-time capacity. It was right after our son was born. Stubborn as I am, I was sure this was not very *practical*. It was risky, really bad timing, and the opposite of safe. But the calling was clear on both of our lives, and so, with much fear and trepidation, we stepped out of the safety of the boat to walk on the water with the same Jesus who walked through the fire with us a few years before.

Weeks after the arrival of Savannah's little brother, we "retired" from teaching and coaching in high schools and entered international sports development full time, working primarily in countries where Jesus has never been known. We resigned our very safe, very secure teaching jobs and started a non-profit to use our skills in sports to build relationships and do our best to represent Christ. We've taught basketball, volleyball, American football, baseball, softball, Ultimate Frisbee, and golf to people in fifteen countries, most of whom have never heard of Jesus. In the fall of 2013, our family spent three months in South East Asia, training a national basketball team and forging a family of sorts with the people there. We work hard at our craft and earn the right to tell our story and God's intervention in it, not because we have an agenda but because we love God and love people. We don't have the right to push our beliefs or judge those of anyone else's, but I pass the word when there's a good sale at Kohl's— why wouldn't I tell people about the best thing I know?

We can't bear the thought of a man or woman going through life without at least hearing about Jesus. Almost everyone we've ever met believes there is some higher power. Creation points to a creator, just as art points to the artist. They just don't know who he is yet.

A few years ago, we went to a country in West Africa and taught basketball in a remote village. After spending hours and hours teaching the rules of the game and developing skills on a makeshift outdoor court with hundreds of young adults in the blazing sun, they invited us to come into their homes and talk. We sat down with a group of elders who, after asking what religion we followed, asked us to explain the story of our god. So we told them how God created the world and a perfect relationship with Himself, man and woman; how we chose another way and distanced ourselves from God; how generations have moved farther and farther away from God; how God's heart breaks at the darkness we chose to live in; how He provided a sacrifice to take our darkness and build a way to return to Him; how Jesus was born and lived and died and was resurrected and paved the way to God; and how following that way leads us back to our Creator and a restored place of eternal fellowship with Him.

After hearing the story, the eldest spoke up and, through a translator, said to us, "For generations, we have known that we must worship something, but we did not know what. So we made idols, and we sacrificed our animals to the idols, and prayed to the idols to protect our children and give us rain so our crops would grow. Now our crops have dried up, and all of our animals are gone, and our children are dying. We were just sitting here under this tree trying to decide what to do about this. And now God has sent you to tell us what to do. Now we know who to worship." He looked around, and all of the other elders nodded their agreement. "From this day on, this village will worship Jesus."

I can't make this stuff up.

God gives us the privilege of seeing him draw people to himself all over the world. We mostly just sit back and watch it happen. But I have to confess, the waters get stormy sometimes. We work in some hard places—some dark and scary corners of the world. A couple of years ago, I sat with two women as they made shea butter, and I explained the story of Jesus while a man stood fifty feet away screaming at us and waving a machete over his head. Our 22-year-old translator told the man he'd have to kill us to keep us from telling the truth about God (though he didn't translate that statement into English until after we left). The two college guys standing behind me were praying like possessed men, and I was trying not to wet my pants. But when I stopped talking, one of the women looked at the man with the machete, and she stood straight up from where they'd been sitting on the ground and said she believed this was true and wanted to become a follower of Jesus. The second one followed her lead a few seconds later. One step of courage leads to another. The bravery we witness is astounding, convicting at the very least.

What we do with our lives is not safe or logical. Our income is never guaranteed, Scott travels a lot, and like I said, we're not always in friendly territory.

But our burden, our passion, is to let the whole world know how good God is, how much He loves us all and wants to know and be known by us. We don't think this knowledge is reserved only for the wealthy or the educated or the religious; it was sent to the *whole* world. And Jesus said to whom much is given, much is required. We have a lot to give back, and a responsibility to use the resources we have to honor God and help others. The best way for us to communicate the message of hope is to use our gifts and tell what God has done in our own lives. It's the truth as best we know it.

But we never could have taken this leap, never would have had the courage to take a step this risky, without knowing firsthand who God is and what he can do. And although it's not always easy or safe or practical, we know we don't do it alone.

During a recent, especially tumultuous season, I was struggling with the size of the waves swelling around us. In an emotional conversation, I asked Scott, "Don't you ever feel like we're dangling over the edge of a balcony on the top of a high-rise? Don't you ever get tired of living on the edge?"

"Yes," he said, "sometimes I do. But I know the strength of the hand that holds me, and I know he won't ever let me go."

Gah.

"Besides," he added, "the view is pretty great up here, don't you think?"

And I have to smile and agree. I guess some would call us crazy. I think we were all made for this. Life out on the water with the Savior by our side—living outside the confines of our fear and pain and pride and self-reliance—it's what we were designed to do.

People live outside the boat in all kinds of ways. Some see a need and make room for foster children in their homes, shouting down their own fears and insufficiencies. Parents step onto rough waters when choosing their kids' educational routes: the one who home-schools out of strong conviction and attention to her child's needs is every bit as obedient as the one who steps past the instinct to shelter and sends their kids to the mission field of public school. Both swim against the currents of opinion and judgment of the world around them. College students take stands of conviction on their campuses, soaked in the saltwater and brine sprayed by atheistic agendas and anti-Christian activists. School teachers overflow with the love of their Jesus in the midst of the restrictions and risks imposed by the authorities. Housewives, businessmen, and retirees sacrifice comfort and safety and status quo to serve and bind the wounds of the poor and broken; they travel to third world countries to feed children, they set up ministries in poverty-stricken pockets of their cities, they befriend and counsel the lost and wounded, and they teach people to read and write. I know dozens of people who choose to follow that still, small voice, who keep their eyes on Jesus when He calls them out of the boat instead of looking at the waves crashing around them and limiting their lives to the confines of a tiny floating vessel. Our lives were not written into existence so that we could build safe little nest eggs for ourselves on our way to heaven, side-stepping discomfort and disappointment and the risks that come from following Jesus to hard places. The point of life is to *overcome* adversity, not avoid it. Life out on the water is the abundant life Jesus talked about. It's watching God do the impossible that convinces me to follow Him.

I never would have had the courage to get out of the boat had I not experienced the mighty hand of my God during the worst of storms. And listen: life on the water isn't easy or safe. But it's where Jesus is. He's not stranded on the shore, not camping out on the top of a mountain, and certainly not hiding out in the house. He's *moving,* pursuing us, motioning for us to join Him outside the boat.

Come.

He will come like a rushing stream . . .

~ Isaiah 59:19b (GW)

CHAPTER 13

KEEP MOVING

Whether you turn to the right or to the left,

your ears will hear a voice behind you saying,

"This is the way; walk in it."

~ Isaiah 30:21

WE SAILED THROUGH THE MAGICAL land of elementary school with all of its wholesome adventures: the first lost tooth, class plays, field trips, holiday parties, digging through the mud pit at Barrier Island. (Okay, I confess: Scott ponied up for that one. He's the fun parent.) And we pressed through the little challenges: multiplication flash cards and charts posted in the bedroom, the infamous science fair projects that seemed like they'd be fun at first but ended up with us both crying, losing the class election, her first B. These are the elementary problems we have to let our kids endure and overcome early on if they're going to survive the bigger ones later.

When Savannah was almost four, we took her to be fitted for a prosthesis. Because she has no hip bone on the left side, the prosthetic leg had a strap that wrapped around her waist to hold it up, and she had to swing her torso to move it forward. That lasted for about a minute and a half. She dragged it across the room a couple of times before ditching it altogether.

"Nope, slows me down," she said. She ripped it off and threw it on the floor and took off, never looking back. I did my best to try to get her to give it a second chance, but she's pretty hard to persuade when her mind is made up about something. The leg stayed in her closet, and when we put our house on the market and scheduled a showing with a real estate agent, it was a little bit of a surprise to the prospective buyers who came over to take a look at the house--and the closets. They didn't come back for a second showing. From then on, we learned to hide it under the bed—until the neighbors' kids came over to play hide-and-seek, which Savannah thought was hilarious. It's a good thing we moved.

Her strong will and weird sense of humor are not traits I always appreciate, especially in a fourteen-year-old, but it helps her in a lot of ways. There's a whole set of difficulties that accompanies having a left leg amputation.

First of all: the staring. My gosh, the staring. My mom always taught me it was rude to stare, so I DO NOT GET THIS. Seriously, I know people are curious, and if you want to sneak a look when we walk by, that's one thing. We'll just pretend we don't notice. But there are the exceptional people who just lack some serious social skills and are a little harder to be patient with. For instance, Savannah and I went to the gas station one Friday after school to get our "Friday treat" (which consists of a glamorous Icee and boiled peanuts), and as we're walking out the door, this grown man practically wails, "OH MY [GOODNESS]! What *happened* to her?" We both looked behind us to see who he was talking to. Again he says, "Oh my [goodness]!" in this melodramatic moan, and I turn to see him gawking at Savannah with his hands on his face and looking like he's about to cry. I swear, you would have thought he actually just witnessed the amputation of her leg.

Awww, man, no . . . don't do this.

He moved toward Savannah like he was going to scoop her up and take her to surgery. Savannah double-stepped it toward the car like a bird evading a cat, and I stepped in between them because *You need to back off, dude.* He stopped and looked at me all distraught and said, "Is she okay? Is she gonna be okay? What happened to her?"

"She's fine," I reassured him with my "be gracious" smile that probably looks more like *You're an idiot*, because that's what I'm actually thinking.

"But—oh my [goodness]," he whined, "what *happened* to her?"

Keep smiling. I took a deep breath.

"She was born with cancer. They removed the tumor. She's very healthy now. Thank you for your concern. She's doing great."

He finally relented and went into the store, and I got in the car with Savannah, who just said, "Seriously?" and turned the radio up.

Grace. Grace. I know people don't mean any harm. I know they're just curious or concerned, so I try to remember that not everybody is used to seeing a girl with one leg on bright green crutches every day. I try to remember that this is our normal, but it's not to the rest of the world. I try to be full of grace and give people the benefit of the doubt, because Lord knows I need that from others. So I try to choose grace.

But some times are harder than others.

Like the time we went into the bathroom at Chuck E. Cheese and I waited by the sinks while Savannah went into the stall, and the little girl who had just finished washing her hands peered around the stall to watch Savannah go in. She turned to me with her face wrinkled up like a Pug and said, "Creepy."

Oh, no she didn't.

I leaned over and looked under the bathroom stalls to make sure nobody else was in the bathroom with us. Then I leaned down toward that little girl's face and said, "Well, you know what? I think *you're* creepy, and you better get out of here and go find your mama and tell her she needs to teach you some manners."

She just shrugged and threw her paper towel on the floor and left.

"Mama? Are you talking to somebody?" Savannah yelled from the end stall.

"Nobody, baby. But hurry up. We need to get out of here."

Before you think I'm all tough and quick on the draw like some Texas Ranger taking down bad guys and dispensing justice, let me tell you that I just about hyperventilated as soon as the girl walked out the door. It's not exactly my style to insult ten-year-olds, and I regretted it as soon as it came out of my mouth. And because I had a pretty good feeling that her mama wouldn't appreciate the advice and we might end up on the *Jerry Springer* show or a *Law & Order* episode, I scurried Savannah out of the bathroom and told Scott we needed to get out of Dodge as fast as possible. He didn't even ask questions because he hates Chuck E. Cheese even more than I do, and we hit the door like we stole something from the prize counter.

It was not my finest moment.

I'd like to use every unpleasant situation as a learning opportunity and teach the world to sing in perfect harmony and all that, but I'd be lying if I told you I don't sometimes want to punch people in the face. When moms send their children over to ask Savannah what happened, explaining that they want their children to learn how to "confront their fears," I want to tell them to go sign up for karate—my daughter is not their kid's *sensei*. She's not an educational tool or an exhibit at the zoo. She's a kid. With feelings. She doesn't like to be pointed at or questioned or stopped on the street so people can take a picture of "such an amazing little girl." How would you like it if I pointed at your most unusual qualities? Or asked if I could take a picture of your kid because I've never seen hair quite so furry or so many freckles on one face before? I want your kid to have social skills too, but please don't use my kid to teach them. She just wants to be normal, like everybody else.

But, usually, we just smile and answer their questions. Because people deserve grace. And I want to teach my kid some things too. I want her to learn to be gracious and patient and to consider others above herself. I want her to try to see things from others' perspectives, to give them the benefit of the doubt, to recognize that people are generally good-hearted and aren't trying to be rude. Because they're not. Most people are so kind, so accepting.

We have so many amazing people in our lives who love Savannah for who she is and don't notice what she isn't. Friends, family, teachers, neighbors, college kids at church—they expect and call out the best in her without making excuses or expecting her to be a superhero. These are the kind of people we want in our daughter's life.

This year, Savannah swam on our high school swim team. It's been her dream since she started swimming at age six. Dorman has about a million students, but there's no middle school or junior varsity swim teams, so she swam on the varsity team as a seventh grader. It was not easy. She worked her tail off, and she didn't win a single race. In fact, she finished last in all but one race. But she learned a ton about working toward a goal, about being a part of a team, and about winning in the small things. I can't tell you how much I appreciated her coaches. I love those people. They were as tough on her as they were on everybody else and encouraged her to do some things she didn't think she could do. She loved every second of it. Because she doesn't want to be *special*; she just wants to be a kid.

In one of the last meets of the season, she was swimming the 100-meter freestyle and was in last place, about ten meters behind her opponent. She was in the outside lane closest to the side of the pool, and when she flip-turned, Coach Raymond stepped up to the side of the pool and walked beside her all the way back down, looking like a fool waving his hands and pointing to the end of the pool, yelling *Go, Savannah, go! You can do this!*

The gap began to close, and I realized I had slowly risen to my feet, standing straight up in the crowd with my hands clasped together like the lady in *The Natural*. My heart was pounding. (Are you having déjà vu? I swear, this stuff happens.)

You're gonna pass her! You can do this! Coach Raymond was barking and swinging his arm toward the finish line, and now the whole team was starting to cheer. I watched all this play out like a movie I was *not* in because my daughter is going to have to start to learn how to live life without me eventually, and I realized this was the beginning of that. But the drama of the moment was swelling, my heart was beating in my throat, and Coach Raymond was practically squatting down and duck-walking to stay in Savannah's ear.

Go, go, go! You're gonna do it! Don't quit! Go!

With about ten meters to go, stroke by determined stroke, Savannah passed the girl in lane two. Her team roared like she'd just won the World Games.

She finished in next-to-last place. And it was glorious. There are some wins that just can't be measured by the lit bulbs of a scoreboard.

We've all grown up a lot. That little baby in the first ten chapters is growing up fast, and we've had to grow up as well. I think back to that young woman who had a baby thirteen years ago, and I hardly recognize her. I just finished rereading the previous chapters, because I haven't in a long time, and sometimes I just need to remember. And I think I don't even know that young mom who wrote the story. She was coming off the high of rescue and settling in to the sweet lull of raising young children and bringing cupcakes to class parties and reading bedtime stories and teaching her babies that Jesus loves all the little children of the world. I read her voice in those pages and I think she sounded so young. I can't remember her much. She was young and scared and didn't know what she was doing.

Wait a minute. Come to think of it, I am *exactly* the same, except not so young. But life has ramped up. God has called us out into deeper waters in so many areas of our lives, but parenting . . . well, nobody told me how hard this job would be. We are full-on into the throes of middle school now, and *I still don't know what I'm doing.* Savannah has an actual countdown of how many days until she can drive. It scares me to death to try to raise two little(ish) people to be courageous and kind and considerate and honest and to be givers to the world instead of takers. Or even just *not* criminals or derelicts.

Most days I'm sure I'm in the remedial parenting class. I look at other people with kids my age who seem to be organized and unflustered and so dang *capable,* who don't forget to pack the lunch or wash the uniform or sign the blasted Friday folder. How, I want to know, did they know how to navigate the middle school car pick-up line the first week while I was straight up having a panic attack in the lane next to them? This parenting thing just does not come naturally for me. I get *way* more wrong than I do right.

But then there's grace.

Right in the middle of failure and frustration and confusion and burning the frozen pizza and setting off the fire alarm again, God steps in and fills the gaps. Sometimes it is seeing another groggy and bleary-eyed mom pulled over by the side of the drop-off lane in the school parking lot with her hair disheveled and still wearing her pajamas and looking in her rear view mirror to watch her child walk into the building, and I raise my fist to her as I cruise by. *I feel you, sister. Solidarity.*

Sometimes grace shows up in a clean shirt I didn't remember folding, or just enough milk in the jug to pour one last glass, or a sale on Gatorade at the end of the month. Sometimes it's a word spoken just right and at just the right time. Sometimes it's in a wise word spoken from the mouths of my own children who I did not know were listening. Sometimes it's in the chocolate chip waffle my son makes me for breakfast in bed, or the fact that my fourteen-year-old daughter still wants me to lie in the bed with her and talk at night. Sometimes it's laughter in the most awkward places.

When she was twelve, Savannah and I were standing in line at the concession stand waiting for my son's baseball game to start, and this little kid walks up to her wearing a jersey and a cap and baseball glove that were way too big for his five-year-old body. He walked in a circle around her, sizing her up, and looked up at her and said, "Hey, what happened to your other leg?"

Without hesitating, Savannah said, "I didn't eat my vegetables when I was little," shaking her head with feigned remorse. The poor kid dropped his lower jaw and his glove at exactly the same time and just stood there gaping as Savannah turned slowly and clicked off on her crutches with a sly, sideways grin.

I looked at the kid, and he looked up at me and said, "For real?" And I said, "You really need to eat your vegetables."

By the time I caught up with her, she was doubled over laughing, and I said, "I cannot believe you just did that."

"Well, it was better than making us both feel awkward," she said. "Plus, his mom will probably be glad." We laughed about it for days.

So to the mother of the traumatized little leaguer who wants broccoli for breakfast every day, my daughter says, "You're welcome."

Life's crazy. You can never be fully prepared for it. And we all have our disabilities. Sometimes they're physical; not every kid was made to be a star athlete or beauty queen or A+ student. And although size and shape and strength will always be a measuring line, we can elevate each other by acknowledging and drawing out deeper beauty and strength.

Sometimes the emotional hurdles are even tougher to overcome. Our insecurities, fears, baggage, trauma, broken relationships, they all take our legs out from under us sometimes. We each walk around with a limp of some sort. Every parent has to find a way to help their kids through their own battles, to recognize their strengths and weaknesses and find their own way. Every parent needs to do the same for themselves too. There's no good way to do any of this without clinging to a God who sees our little bitty selves and the whole picture at the same time. I just don't have enough perspective sometimes.

I think maybe it's the having a limp that keeps us from getting too far ahead of ourselves and God. I can't find a better way to live or love or forgive or play or serve than staying close to God. I need Him. There's a good lesson in Jacob's wrestling with the Lord in the desert; Jacob walked away with a limp, but there was no forgetting he had spent some serious time with God. More than anything, I want my children to experience the presence and power of God in their everyday lives. And we adults have to do the same because *Lord knows* we do not have this thing figured out.

So I'm still just trying to stay close. I'm just listening with all my might to a heart that loves me and my children even more than I do, to the One who has perspective on all this nonsense and has plans far better than my own. It takes intentionality to hear that voice.

When I was in high school, I ran the 800-meter event on the track team. My dad helped me train, and during my senior year, we set a goal to qualify for the state meet. But I was having a hard time figuring out how to time my kick on the last turn. Sometimes I'd kick too soon and run out of steam before the finish line, sometimes too late and not have enough time to catch the lead runners. So about halfway through the season, my daddy started signaling when I should make my move. At about the 200-meter mark, he would cup his hands together and yell as loudly as he could, *Now, Wendy, NOW!* He could see the race from a better perspective than I could see it: he didn't panic when he heard footsteps right behind, or when the runner in front seemed to be getting too far of a lead. My dad could see exactly when the time was right, and I started tuning out all the other sounds and distractions around me and listened for that *one* voice in the crowd: *Now, Wendy, NOW!*

I won third place in the state meet that year, and at the Upper-State meet, I came from behind because my daddy gave me the cue a little earlier than usual—he knew I'd need a little more juice for that finish. I passed the number one runner in the last twenty meters of the race, using up every shred of strength I had, and literally fell over the finish line in first place, face-planting on the asphalt. My dad was there to pick me up and celebrate the victory. Later that night, I went to the prom wearing a fresh streak of road-rash across my face. It was so worth it.

This is how I want to live and love and raise my children: as hard and as well as I can, listening to the *one* voice that has perspective and my best interests at heart among the noise of the crowds, and finishing well. Sometimes I win, and sometimes I don't. But you've got to keep moving forward.

I've watched my daughter take some nasty falls. She walks with straight-arm crutches and wields them like a boss most days, but she's had some mean wipe-outs. Wet floors are tricky. So are stairs. Chair legs jump out of nowhere and trip her up. Getting in and out of our mini-van carrying a backpack and lunchbox and trombone case took some time to figure out. (And, yes, she picked the trombone, of all the instruments in the band or orchestra, because there is no taking the easy route for her. Ever.) Slick pool decks make me a nervous wreck, and I have to hold my breath (and my tongue) and look away when she ditches the crutches and skips pogo-style across the tile on her bare foot. But she never thinks twice about it. She just goes for it, and rolls her eyes at me for worrying. She's trying to get somewhere, you know? She doesn't dwell much on fear or mistakes or the endless possibilities of bad things that could happen, because really, what good does it do anyway? As she would say, in her middle school vernacular, "Ain't nobody got time for dat!" Sigh.

My daughter is still teaching me much about life. Sometimes you fall. Sometimes you sit and cry about it for a little while; that's allowed. Sometimes you laugh it off and hope nobody saw. Sometimes you acknowledge your own shortcomings and take more care on slippery floors or just don't go that way again. Everybody stumbles, whether they walk on crutches or not. Some falls have greater consequences than others. But always, there's grace, right in the middle of it.

We don't expect each other to be perfect around here. This is the first time she's ever been a teenager, and this is the first time I've ever been the parent of a teenager. So we give and ask for a lot of grace. Daily, it seems, I have to reel it all in, take a deep breath, and say, "Hey, I've never done this before. Give me a break." And I remind myself to give the same.

Life is not easy for an amputee. But it's not easy for anybody else either. We all have a different limp. We all have to overcome our own missing limbs. Maybe a father or mother was absent in your life. Maybe there's an empty space where you thought a mate would be by now, or a big gaping hole a divorce or death left behind. Maybe it's courage or confidence or conviction or children or compassion you're lacking. Limited education, financial struggles, depression, loneliness, abuse, disapproval, rejection: all these things make us feel less than whole, no matter what image we may present to the world. But look around. Really look, and listen, to the people you encounter. We *all* feel that way. Everybody's got a gap, a hole, a hollow where doubt and fear and confusion and anger and frustration settle in and wreak their havoc. Everybody you meet is fighting a battle, even the ones who seem to have it all together. It is the one thing we all have in common: no one ever feels like enough. There's always something missing.

And I wonder if that gap, that space tucked away down deep, might be God's way of making room for Himself. A place to unfold grace and lay it out over the barren spaces like a hand-made quilt. A place to hear God say, *This is how I've made you: every inch of you I stitched by hand. Where you are weak, I am strong.* Maybe He reserves that empty room for Himself so that when the hurdles and falls come, there is a place to huddle together with Him that is void of the clutter of pride, ambition, and self-reliance: an unadorned temple where we can come without pretense or production. It's a place where He can remind us that we're not alone, that everyone we meet has the same empty spot, just perhaps in another place. This helps me to see people clearly, helps me look at people as fellow amputees instead of competition. Those empty spots remind me to keep grace in the middle of it all. Because no one has it all together. No one.

When people tell me how amazing my daughter is, I say "thank you" because I know they are right, but I also know about the Battle Royale we had in the car that morning when she threatened to use her crutch as a lethal weapon against her brother and beat him senseless over who got to ride in the front seat last. She's not perfect. Frankly, she and we get more attention than we want or deserve. We're just people, just a regular family trying to live regular lives. But maybe we do have a greater sense of purpose because we have so much to be thankful for. We've been given much.

Most of us have a tendency to dwell on what we don't have instead of the abilities and blessings right in front of us. So if there's a common disability, I think it's blindness to our own capabilities and potential. It's losing sight of the endless possibilities that were sown into us at our custom creation. It's forgetting that we were made to walk on water, not cower at the sound of thunder.

Balancing on the rocks at Edisto Island

When most people see my daughter, they see a girl missing a leg. I see my daughter, whom I love more than my own life. I see a girl whose future is full of *anything*. She has so much of God yet to discover. He's revealing Himself one step at a time, as He does for us all. And surely, there will be more difficult roads where she'll have to lean on Him a little harder. She'll stumble and fall sometimes, just like all of us, because life is hard. But Savannah reminds me constantly of the one trait that seems to determine one's ability to succeed in this life: *resilience*.

When she falls, she gets up and moves on. And so can you.

CHAPTER 14

THROUGH SAVANNAH'S EYES

HEY, GUYS, IT'S ME, SAVANNAH. I was asked to write a chapter giving my side of this whole adventure, and to be honest with you, I think it's going to be fun. So let's get started, shall we?

It's 2015 and I am now fourteen and in the eighth grade, and that's a struggle on its own, with the zits and the fitting in and all of that junk. But if you think that's tough, add in the fact that I'm the only person in the school who has to worry about getting a lunch tray to the table without it spilling everywhere, or wet floors that could cause my crutches to slip out from under me, or apologizing when someone lands on their face because they've tripped over my crutches sticking out from under my desk in class.

Speaking of crutches, let me please make it very clear that the word is CRUTCHES not CRUNCHES. Crunches are the exercise, guys. Seriously, people. Every time someone says they like my "crunches," I'm just like, "What?" It stumps me every time. But it's cool, at least I'm not still bombarded with the usual, "What's up with your leg?" or the, "Oh my gosh, are you okay?" or the occasional, "What the heck happened to you?" Nobody at school or church treats me any differently or makes a big deal about it anymore. I mean, I'll get a couple of questions here and there from those who are a little curious because they don't know all the details.

When I get off campus or leave church, it's a whole 'nother ball game. Out in the real world, there are little kids who will ask me questions on how and why my body looks the way it does, the mothers who shove their kids my way and then scurry away like I can't see what they're up to, or—my personal favorite—the erratic man or woman who lacks every social skill in the book and runs up to me freaking out as if I were on fire or who just stops and stares as I walk by. That's the world I live in, folks.

Not everyone reacts to me badly; that's not what I'm trying to say. I'm just saying it matters what you say and do to people because it can affect them in the long run. No, not everything is bad. There's a lot of good in it too, like having an elderly woman compliment me on how well I move around, or just simply a stranger thanking me for holding the door and then holding the next one for me. Simple things like that make the world better for everyone.

I'm not as different as people might think I am. I still go through the whole teenager phase. I still worry about pimples and my hair and if I make good grades (because I know if I don't, I'll be in a heap of trouble). See, I'm just the same as you are, as everyone else. We're all the same; we just get to the same place by different roads.

People are pretty much the same on the inside. I have fears and doubts and worries, and I like to laugh and be loved . . . just like you. I'm a regular person, just a different kind of regular.

I asked some of my friends recently if they had any questions about me that they've always wanted to know but didn't want to ask. So here's what inquiring minds wanted to know.

Q: Did you use crutches all of your life?

A: No, I had a walker with a horn and everything until I was about three or four and got tiny little crutches.

Q: Do you ever wonder what it would be like to have two legs?

A: Sometimes, like when I put on my shoe and think about how much longer it would take to put a whole other shoe on. Even with one shoe, I'm still late for school every morning. Same is true for shaving my leg—how do you two-legged people do it? I would like to be able to scratch my nose and walk at the same time, though. It's little things.

Q: What do you do to your jeans so the left leg doesn't hang?

A: Good question! This might seem difficult, but I promise it's not. If my mom and I can figure these things out, anyone can, y'all. So here's the answer: I stick my arm through the left leg, pull it inside-out and push it through the right leg. Like my mom says, there's no playbook for this "one leg" thing, so we just figure it out as we go.

There are actually some perks to only having one leg (besides not having to shave two of them). For instance, we found out that Disney has a policy that people with disabilities don't have to wait in line. We didn't know this, but, hey, rules are rules, and my parents taught me to obey authority, so when the Disney line people came and took us to the front, all I could think was *Score!*

Gearing up before a high school swim meet

My mom mentioned once or twice that I swim for my high school swim team, and I know she told stories about last season, but this season was different from last year: new sets, new teammates, new goals, new everything. The one thing that wasn't new was the fact that I hadn't won a single race yet. And this is the moment where I get to tell you I finally won a race! . . . but I'd be lying. No, I still haven't won yet, but I did accomplish something almost equivalent to winning: I finished the 500 meter event. Now, for those of you who don't know how many laps that is (like my mom), it's twenty. Twenty laps. I decided to compete in this event because, 1) I'm not very fast, and this is more of an endurance event, and 2) my mom said this could be my present to her for her birthday since the meet was on September 18, which is my birthday and two days before hers.

As you can probably tell by now, I decided to take on the challenge. So I got ready for the race all week, and by "got ready," I mean I swam and tried my hardest not to talk myself out of it because that's a lot of laps, people. Nevertheless, I found myself on the block, waiting on the buzzer that would cue me to jump into the water. There I went, plunging myself into the water. I wasn't expecting to win; I really just wanted to finish. I paced myself so I had enough energy to complete the race and thought I was doing okay. Then my arms started to get tired, and I felt myself slowing down. But as I turned to breathe, I saw my coach, Jim Raymond, and my teammate, Andy Cockerell, yelling in the chaos of people for me to "Go!" So I kept going, and as soon as I flip-turned, there were Coach Raymond and Andy walking beside me on the side of the pool again, staying in eye-shot, so I wouldn't stop. And sure enough, I didn't. I kept at it, and then I realized I was on my last lap. By that time, I was going full-speed because I knew I was going to make it! I ended up in second place, barely in front of the girl in the lane on my right, but I couldn't even celebrate because I was so tired.

That was one of the hardest things I've ever done, but I accomplished it with practice and a whole lot of encouragement. Most of all, it took strength, and I'm not trying to say I've got a whole bunch of it, but I know where my strength comes from. It comes from God. He's the One you go to when you're barely hanging in there or even when your life feels perfect. God's the One you can go to when your dad leaves or your mom loses her job or friends turn their back on you or life just punches you in the face (those things haven't happened to me, but I know people it has happened to, and I hope they're reading this). Life's hard sometimes; it is for everybody. We all have our bad days, and bad things happen to all of us. But when you feel weak, God's got your back; all you have to do is ask for strength. Psalm 18:32 says, "It is God who arms me with strength and keeps my way secure." If you just ask God to give you a little boost, He'll be there for you. Sometimes you might have to wait a little while, but He's got a reason for what He does. You might not see the reason, but it's there. Just wait and see.

I have no memory of any of the procedures or medicines or tears or any of the things that happened early in my life. All I have to go by are the stories from all of the loving people that were by my side the entire time. I do, however, hate apple juice, and my mom says it's because they would put some nasty tasting medicine in it.

I know that my parents had to make a lot of difficult decisions in my earlier life. Some were pretty easy, and some were pretty hard. For instance, they had to first decide if they were going to keep me. I know that sounds like a terrible thing to have to think about, but they had to think through the effects keeping me would have. The doctors told them about all the things that could've been wrong with me, and none of them were proven to be true. . . well, except the obvious. They also had to figure out if they were going to keep the remaining part of my leg or remove it. They had to try to think through my entire life and how this would affect me in the long run. Knowing the decisions they had to make and how hard it was for them makes me wonder how I would react to something like that and shows me how strong and brave they were. They were young and had the rest of their lives to live. Having a child that might have to be taken care of 24/7 would be difficult on a couple that young, but they took a chance against all of the doctors and believed in me and God's plan.

I sometimes get asked what I think God's plan is for me. I constantly hear the phrase, "God's got a plan for you," and I know that, but y'all, I'm only fourteen: I don't know what that is yet. Maybe the plan is for me to go and share the gospel to every country on the planet, or maybe to swim in the Paralympics, or maybe it's that I just need to stay in Spartanburg. I don't know what God's plan is yet, but that's okay because I've got a while to figure it out. But He sure did go to a lot of trouble to get me to this point, so it must be a pretty good one. I'll just have to trust Him to show me, one step at a time.

My grace is sufficient for you, for my power
is made perfect in weakness.

~ 2 Corinthians 12:9b

ACKNOWLEDGEMENTS

I know full well that no accomplishment comes without the support of good people, and I am richly blessed to have some good ones in my life.

To Scott . . . I love your guts out. Thank you for always believing in me, for being strong enough for both of us, and for not only *not* complaining, but cheering me on during the long hours required to finish this endeavor.

To my children, Savannah and JP, who endured tons of Ramen noodles and frozen pizzas and never complained while I worked on this. You're my heroes; you teach me to be brave.

To my parents, who have supported me in everything I've ever wanted to do in life: you've taught me that anything is possible with a little courage and a lot of work. Thank you for the example you've set.

To the incredible doctors, nurses, medical staff, and volunteers at Greenville Hospital, Duke Medical Center, Greenville Shriners Hospital, and Cincinnati Children's Hospital: we cannot thank you enough for the care you gave us. You are heroes every day.

Many thanks to our family and friends who have loved us and supported us, walked with us through the hardest days, and continue to encourage me to tell this story.

To my pastor and my First North family: thank you for being the hands and feet of Christ, for holding our arms up over the battlefield.

And to Tim and the team at Ambassador International: thanks for taking a chance on me and helping me tell this story.

Finally, to God the Father, whose beautiful story weaves together all of our smaller ones: all gratitude and praise and glory forever.

I am blessed far beyond what I deserve.

ABOUT THE AUTHOR

Wendy Duke lives in South Carolina with her husband and two children. She works with her husband in international sports development, using their backgrounds in coaching and telling their story throughout the world. When she's not traveling, she is a Bible teacher, speaker, blogger, sports junkie, and middle school chauffeur.

You can check out her blog at www.wendyduke.net.

For more information about

Wendy Duke

and
Grace in the Middle
please visit:

www.wendyduke.net
wendy@wendyduke.net
@WendyDuke32
www.facebook.com/wendymorrowduke

For more information about
AMBASSADOR INTERNATIONAL
please visit:

www.ambassador-international.com
@AmbassadorIntl
www.facebook.com/AmbassadorIntl